FIVE ON A HIKE TOGETHER

FIVE ON
A HIKE
TOGETHER

Enid Blyton

Hodder
Children's
Books

a division of Hodder Headline plc

First published in Great Britain in 1951
by Hodder and Stoughton

This edition 1991

The right of Enid Blyton to be identified as the Author of
the Work has been asserted by her in accordance with the
Copyright, Designs and Patents Act 1988.

10

A catalogue record for this book is available from the
British Library

ISBN 0 340 54884 3

Printed and bound in Great Britain by
Caledonian International Book Manufacturing Ltd, Glasgow

Hodder Children's Books
A division of Hodder Headline plc
338 Euston Road
London NW1 3BH

Contents

1 A letter from Julian

'Anne!' shouted George, running after her cousin as she went along to her classroom. 'Anne! I've just been down to the letterboard and there's a letter from your brother Julian. I've brought it for you.'

Anne stopped. 'Oh thanks,' she said. 'What *can* Julian want? He only wrote a few days ago – it's most extraordinary for him to write again so soon. It must be something important.'

'Well, open it and see,' said George. 'Hurry up – I've got a maths class to go to.'

Anne ripped open the envelope. She pulled out a sheet of notepaper and read it quickly. She looked up at George, her eyes shining.

'George! Julian and Dick have got a few days off at our half-term weekend! Somebody's won a wonderful scholarship or something, and the boys have got two days tacked on to a weekend to celebrate! They want us to join them in a hike, and all go off together.'

'What a glorious idea!' said George. 'Good old Julian. I bet he thought of that. Let's read the letter, Anne.'

But before she could read it a mistress came along. 'Georgina! You should be in class – and you too, Anne.'

George scowled. She hated to be called by her full name. She went off without a word. Anne tucked the letter into her pocket and rushed off joyfully. Half-term with her brothers, Julian and Dick – and with George and Timmy the dog. Could anything be better?

She and George talked about it again after morning school. 'We get from Friday morning till Tuesday,' said George. 'The boys are getting the same. What luck! They don't usually have a half-term in the winter term.'

'They can't go home because the painters are in our house,' said Anne. 'That's why I was going home with you, of course. But I'm sure your mother won't mind if we go off with the boys. Your father never likes us in the middle of the term.'

'No, he doesn't,' said George. 'He's always deep in the middle of some wonderful idea, and he hates to be disturbed. It will suit everyone if we go off on a hike.'

'Julian says he will telephone to us tonight and arrange everything,' said Anne. 'I hope it will be a nice fine weekend. It will still be October, so there's a chance of a bit of warm sunshine.'

'The woods will be beautiful,' said George. 'And won't Timmy enjoy himself. Let's go and tell him the news.'

The boarding-school that the two girls were at was one that allowed the children to bring their own pets to school. There were kennels down in the yard for various dogs, and Timmy lived there during term-time. The two girls went to get him.

He heard their footsteps at once and began to bark excitedly. He scraped at the gate of the kennel yard, wishing for the thousandth time that he could find out how to open it.

He flung himself on the two girls, licking and pawing and barking.

'Silly dog. Mad dog!' said George, and thumped his back affectionately. 'Listen, Tim – we're going off for the weekend with Julian and Dick! What do you think of that? We're going on a hike, so you'll love it. All through the woods and up the hills and goodness knows where!'

Timmy seemed to understand every word. He cocked up his ears, put his head on one side and listened intently while George was speaking.

'Woof,' he said, at the end, as if he approved thoroughly. Then off he went with the girls for his walk, his plumy tail wagging happily. He didn't like term-time nearly as much as the holidays – but he was quite prepared to put up with kennel life so long as he could be near his beloved George.

Julian rang up that night as he had promised. He had got everything planned already. Anne listened, thrilled.

'It sounds super,' she said. 'Yes – we can meet where you say, and we'll be there as near as we can on time. Anyway, we can wait about if you others aren't there. Yes – we'll bring the things you say. Oh Julian, won't it be fun?'

'What's he say?' asked George impatiently when at last Anne put the receiver down. 'You might have let me have a word with Julian. I wanted to tell him all about Timmy.'

'He doesn't want to waste an expensive telephone call listening to you raving about Timmy,' said Anne. 'He asked how he was and I said "fine", and that's all he wanted to know about Tim. He's made all the arrangements. I'll tell you what they are.'

The girls went off to a corner of their common-room and sat down. Timmy was there too. He was allowed in at certain times, and so were three other dogs belonging to the girls. Each dog behaved well – he knew that if he didn't he would be taken back to the kennels at once!

'Julian says that he and Dick can get off immediately after breakfast,' said Anne. 'So can we, so that's all right. He says we've got to take very little with us – just night things, toothbrush, hairbrush and flannel and a rolled-up mac. And any biscuits or chocolate we can buy. Have you any money left?'

'A bit,' said George. 'Not much. Enough to buy a few bars of chocolate, I think. Anyway, you've got all the biscuits your mother sent last week. We can take some of those.'

'Yes. And the barley sugar one of my aunts sent,' said Anne. 'But Julian says we're not to take much because this is to be a proper hike, and we'll get tired if we have to carry a heavy load. Oh, he said put in two pairs of extra socks.'

'Right,' said George, and she patted Timmy who was lying close beside her. 'There's going to be a long walky-walk, Tim. Won't you love that!'

Timmy grunted comfortably. He wondered if there would be any rabbits on the walk. A walk wasn't really exciting unless there were rabbits all over the place. Timmy thought it was a pity that rabbits were allowed to live down holes. They always disappeared most unfairly just when he had nearly caught one!

Anne and George went to see their house-mistress to tell her that they were not going to Kirrin Cottage after all, but were going walking.

'My brother says he has written to you,' said Anne. 'So you'll know all about it tomorrow, Miss Peters. And George's mother will be writing too. We can go, can't we?'

'Oh, yes – it will be a lovely half-term for you!' said

Miss Peters. 'Especially if this sunny weather lasts. Where are you going?'

'Over the moors,' said Anne. 'In the very loneliest, most deserted parts that Julian can find! We might see deer and wild ponies and perhaps even a few badgers. We shall walk and walk.'

'But where will you sleep if the parts you are going to are so very lonely?' asked Miss Peters.

'Oh Julian is arranging all that,' said George. 'He's been looking up little inns and farmhouses on the map, and we shall make for those at night. It will be too cold to sleep out of doors.'

'It certainly will!' said Miss Peters. 'Well don't get into trouble, that's all. I know what you five are when you get together. I imagine Timmy is going with you too?'

'Of *course*!' said George. 'I wouldn't go if he didn't go! I couldn't leave him here alone.'

The two girls got their things ready as Friday came near. The biscuits were taken out of the tin and put into paper bags. The barley sugar was put into a bag too, and the bars of chocolate.

Both girls had rucksacks with straps for their shoulders. They packed and repacked them several times. One by one more and more things were added. Anne felt she must take a book to read. George said they must each take a torch with a new battery.

'And what about biscuits for Timmy?' she said. 'I simply must take something for him. He'd like a bone too – a big one that he can chew and chew and that I can put back into the bag for another time.'

'Well, let me carry all the biscuits and chocolate then if you're going to put a smelly old bone into your bag,' said Anne. 'I don't see why you want to take *anything* for Timmy – he can always have something to eat when we do – wherever we have a meal.'

George decided not to take the bone. She had fetched one from his kennel, and it certainly was big and heavy, and equally certainly it was smelly. She took it back to the kennel again, Timmy following her rather puzzled. Why keep carrying his bone here and there? He didn't approve at all.

It seemed a long time till Friday, but at last it came. Both girls woke up very early indeed. George was out in the kennels before breakfast, brushing and combing Timmy to make him look spruce and tidy for Julian and Dick. He knew it was the day they were to set off and he was as excited as the two girls.

'We'd better eat a good breakfast,' said Anne. 'We might have to wait some time before our next meal. Let's slip off immediately after breakfast. It's lovely to feel free of school and bells and time-tables – but I shan't feel *really* free till I'm outside the school grounds!'

They ate an enormous breakfast though really they were too excited to want much. Then they got their rucksacks, ready-packed the night before, said good-bye to Miss Peters, and went to fetch Timmy.

He was waiting impatiently for them, and barked madly when they came near. In a trice he was out of his kennel-yard and capering round them, almost tripping them up.

'Good-bye, Anne and George!' yelled one of their friends. 'Have a good time on your hike – and it's no good coming back on Tuesday and telling us you've had one of your usual hair-raising adventures, because we just shan't believe it!'

'Woof,' said Tommy. 'Woof, woof!' Which meant that *he* was going to have adventures with hundreds of rabbits, anyway!

2   Setting off

Julian and Dick were also on their way, very pleased to have such an unexpectedly long weekend.

'I never liked Willis or Johnson much,' said Dick, as they walked out of the school grounds. 'Awful swotters they were – never had any time for games or fun. But I take my hat off to them today! Because of their swotting they've won medals and scholarships and goodness knows what – and we've got a weekend off in celebration! Good old Willis and Johnson!'

'Hear hear,' said Dick. 'But I bet they'll sit in a corner with their books all the weekend – they won't know if it's a brilliant day like this, or pouring with rain like yesterday! Poor mutts!'

'They'd hate to go off on a hike,' said Julian. 'It would be utter misery to them. Do you remember how awful Johnson was at rugger? He never knew which goal he was playing against – always ran the wrong way!'

'Yes. But he must have got terrific brains,' said Dick. 'Why are we talking about Willis and Johnson? I can think of plenty of more interesting things. Anne and George, for instance – and old Tim. I hope they'll manage to get off in time all right.'

Julian had carefully looked up a large-scale map of the moors that lay between the two schools that he and the girls went to. They were vast stretches of lonely heathery land, dotted with farms here and there, with a few small cottages, and some inns.

'We'll keep right off the main roads, and the second-and third-grades,' he said. 'We'll take the little lanes and paths. I wonder what Timmy will say if we see deer. He'll wonder what in the world they are!'

'He'll only be interested in rabbits,' said Dick. 'I hope he's not as fat as he was last hols. I think we must have given him too many ice-creams and too much chocolate!'

'Well, he won't get that in term-time!' said Julian. 'The girls don't get as much pocket money as we do. Buck up – there's the bus!'

They ran for the little country bus that rumbled along the country lanes, taking people to market, or to the tiny villages that lay here and there tucked away in the moor. It stopped most obligingly for them, and they leapt in.

'Ha! Running away from school?' said the conductor. 'Have to report you, you know!'

'Very funny,' said Julian, bored at this joke, which the conductor produced regularly every time a boy got on board with a rucksack over his shoulders.

They had to get out at the next village and cut across country to get to another bus route. They managed to catch a bus there easily and settled down comfortably in their seats. It was half an hour's run from there to where they had planned to meet the girls.

'Here you are, young sirs,' called the conductor, as the bus ran into a village. It had a wide green on which geese cackled, and a small pond for ducks. 'You wanted Pippin Village, didn't you? We don't go any farther – we just turn round and go back.'

'Thanks,' said the boys and got out. 'Now – are the girls here or not?' said Julian. 'They have to walk from a tiny railway station about two miles away.'

They were not there. Julian and Dick went to have a drink of orangeade at the village store. They had hardly finished when they saw the two girls looking in at the door.

'Julian! Dick! We guessed you'd be eating or drinking!' said Anne, and she rushed at her brothers. 'We came as quickly as we could. The engine broke down – it was such a funny little train! All the passengers got out and advised the engine-driver what to do!'

'Hallo!' said Julian, and gave Anne a hug. He was very fond of his young sister. 'Hallo, George! My, you've grown fat, haven't you?'

'I have not,' said George, indignantly. 'And Timmy isn't fat either, so don't tell him he is.'

'Julian's pulling your leg as usual,' said Dick, giving George a friendly slap on the back. 'All the same, you've grown a bit – you'll soon be as tall as I am. Hallo, Timmy! Good dog, fine dog! Tongue as wet as usual? Yes, it is! I never knew a dog with a wetter tongue than yours!'

Timmy went nearly mad with joy at being with all four of his friends. He leapt round them, barking, wagging his long tail and sending a pile of tins crashing to the floor in his delight.

'Now, now!' said the shop-woman, emerging from a dark little room at the back. 'Take that dog out. He's gone mad!'

'Don't you girls want a drink of ginger-beer or something?' asked Julian, getting hold of Timmy's collar. 'You'd better, because we don't want to have to carry heavy bottles of drinkables with us.'

'Where are we going to set off to?' asked George. 'Yes, I'd like ginger-beer please. Get down, Timmy. Anyone would think you'd been away from Julian and Dick for at least ten years!'

'It probably does seem like ten years to him,' said Anne. 'I say – are those sandwiches?'

She pointed to a ledge at the back of the counter. There was a little pile of sandwiches there, looking most appetising.

'Yes, they're sandwiches, Miss,' said the shop-woman, opening two bottles of ginger-beer. 'I've made them for my son who works over at Blackbush Farm – he'll be in for them soon.'

'I suppose you couldn't make *us* some, could you?' asked Julian. 'We wouldn't need to bother about trying to get to some village at lunch time then. They look jolly good.'

'Yes. I can make you all you want,' said the shop-woman, putting two glasses down in front of the girls. 'What do you want – cheese, egg, ham or pork?'

'Well – we'd like some of all of those,' said Julian. 'The bread looks so nice too.'

'I make it myself,' said the woman, pleased. 'All right – I'll go and make you some. You tell me if anyone comes into the shop while I'm gone.'

She disappeared. 'That's good,' said Julian. 'If she makes plenty of those we can avoid villages all day and have a really good day of exploration – treading where no foot has trod before and all that!'

'How many can you manage each?' asked the woman, suddenly reappearing. 'My son, he has six – that's twelve rounds of bread.'

'Well – could you manage eight sandwiches for each of us?' said Julian. The woman looked astonished. 'It's to last us all day,' he explained, and she nodded and disappeared again.

'That's a nice little sum for her,' said Anne. 'Eight sandwiches each, making sixteen rounds of bread – for four people!'

'Well, let's hope she's got a bread-cutting machine!' said Dick. 'Or we'll be here for keeps! Hallo – who's this?'

A tall man appeared at the entrance of the shop, a bicycle in his hand. 'Ma!' he called.

The children guessed who he was at once – the son who worked over at Blackbush Farm. He had come for his sandwiches!

'Your mother is hard at work cutting sixty-four rounds of bread,' said Dick. 'Shall I get her for you?'

'No. I'm in a hurry,' said the man and he set his bicycle by the door, came in, reached over the counter for his sandwiches and then went back to his bicycle.

'Tell my mother I've been in,' he said. 'And you might tell her I'll be late home today – got to take some stuff to the prison.'

He was off at once, sailing away down the road on his bicycle. The old woman suddenly came in, a knife in one hand, a loaf in the other.

'Did I hear Jim?' she said. 'Oh yes – he's got his sandwiches. You should have told me he was in!'

'He said he was in a hurry,' explained Julian. 'And he said we were to tell you he'd be late today because he had to take some stuff to the prison.'

'I've got another son there,' said the woman. The four looked at her. Did she mean he was a prisoner? And what prison?

She guessed their thoughts and smiled. 'Oh, my Tom isn't a prisoner!' she said. 'He's a warder – a fine fellow. Not a nice job there though – I'm always afraid of those men in prison – a fierce lot, a bad lot!'

'Yes – I've heard there is a big prison on this moor,' said Julian. 'It's marked on our map too. We're not going near it, of course.'

'No. Don't you take the girls near there,' said the

woman, disappearing again. 'If I don't get on with your sandwiches you'll not have them before tomorrow morning.'

Only one customer came in while the children were waiting – a solemn old man smoking a clay pipe. He looked round the shop, couldn't see the woman, took a packet of blancmange powder, which he slipped into his pocket, and put the money down on the counter.

'Tell 'er when 'er comes,' he mumbled with his pipe still in his mouth, and out he shuffled. Timmy growled. The old man smelt very unwashed and Timmy didn't like him.

At last the sandwiches were finished and the old woman appeared again. She had packed them up neatly in four parcels of grease-proof paper, and had pencilled on each what they were. Julian read what she had written and winked at the others.

'My word – we're in for a grand time!' he said. 'Cheese, Pork, Ham and Egg – and what's this?'

'Oh, that's four slices of my home-made fruit cake,' said the old woman. 'I'm not charging you for that. It's just so that you can taste it!'

'It looks like half the cake!' said Julian, touched. 'But we shall pay for it, with many thanks. How much is all that?'

She told him. Julian put down the money and added five pence for the cake. 'There you are, and many thanks,' he said. 'And that money there was left by an old fellow with a clay pipe who took a packet of blancmange powder.'

'That would be Old Gupps,' said the woman. 'Well, I hope you'll enjoy your tour. Come back here if you want any more sandwiches cut! If you eat all those today you won't do badly!'

'Woof,' said Timmy, hoping that he too would

share a few. The woman produced a bone for him, and he took it up in his mouth.

'Thanks!' Julian said. 'Come on – now we'll really start!'

3 Across the countryside

They set off at last, Timmy running in front. School already seemed far behind them. The October sun shone down warmly, and the trees in the village glowed yellow and red and golden, dressed in their autumn colourings. A few leaves floated down in the breeze, but not until there was a real frost would many come whirling down.

'It's a heavenly day,' said George. 'I wish I hadn't got my blazer on. I'm cooked already.'

'Well, take it off and carry it over your shoulder,' said Julian. 'I'm going to do the same. Our jerseys are quite warm enough today!'

They took off their thick blazers and carried them. Each of them had a rucksack, a mac rolled up tightly and tied to it, and now a blazer to carry. But none of them noticed the weight at the outset of their day.

'I'm glad you girls took my advice and wore your thickest shoes,' said Julian, looking with approval at their brogues. 'Some of our walking may be wet. Have you got changes of socks?'

'Yes. We brought everything you told us to,' said Anne. 'Your rucksack looks a bit fuller than ours, Ju!'

'Well, I've got maps and things in it,' said Julian. 'It's a strange place, this moor – miles and miles and miles of it! Strange names on it too – Blind Valley – Rabbit Hill – Lost Lake – Coney Copse!'

'Rabbit Hill! Timmy would love that,' said George,

and Timmy pricked up his ears. Rabbits? Ah, that was the kind of place he liked!

'Well, actually we're going towards Rabbit Hill now,' said Julian. 'And after that there's Coney Copse, and as coney is a country word for rabbit, Timmy ought to enjoy himself!'

'Woof,' said Timmy joyfully and bounded ahead. He felt very happy. His four friends were with him, their rucksacks were full of delicious-smelling sandwiches, and a long, long walk lay ahead, teeming, he hoped with rabbits!

It was lovely walking along in the sun. They soon left the little village behind and took a winding lane. The hedges on either side became so high that the four couldn't see over the tops at all.

'What a sunken lane!' said Dick. 'I feel as if I'm walking in a tunnel! And how narrow! I wouldn't like to drive a car along this lane. If I met another car I might have to back for miles!'

'We shan't meet anyone much,' said Julian. 'It's only in the summer that cars come along these lanes – people on holiday, touring round the countryside. Look – we take that path now – it leads to Rabbit Hill, according to the map!'

They climbed over a stile in the high hedge and walked over a field towards a curious little hill. Timmy suddenly went mad with excitement. He could smell rabbits – and he could see them too!

'You don't often see so many rabbits out in the daytime,' said George, surprised. 'Big ones and little ones too – what a scampering.'

They came to the hill and sat down quietly to watch the rabbits. But it was quite impossible to make Timmy do the same. The sight and smell of so many made him quite wild. He pulled away from George's hand and went bounding madly up the hill, scattering rabbits by the dozen.

'Timmy!' yelled George, but for once Timmy paid no attention. He rushed here and rushed there, getting very angry as first one rabbit and then another neatly popped down a hole.

'It's no use calling him,' said Dick. 'He won't catch one, anyway – see how nippy they are. It's my belief they're having a game with our Timmy!'

It did look rather like it. As soon as Timmy had chased two or three rabbits down one hole, a few more would pop up from another behind him. The children laughed. It was as good as a pantomime.

'Where do you mean to have lunch?' asked Anne. 'If we stay here much longer I shall really have to have something to eat – and it's not nearly time yet. I wish I didn't always feel so hungry in the open air.'

'Well, come on then,' said Julian. 'We've got some way to go before we get to our lunch-place. I've made a pretty good time-table of our tour – we're going to go all round the moors and finish at the place we started at! I've really marked it all out pretty well.'

'Do we sleep at farmhouses or something at night?' asked George. 'I should like that. Will they mind having us, do you think? Or do we go to inns?'

'Farmhouses for two nights and inns for the other nights,' said Julian. 'I've marked them all.'

They went up Rabbit Hill and down the other side. There were just as many rabbits there. Timmy chased them till he panted like an engine going uphill! His tongue hung out, dripping wet.

'You've had enough, Tim,' said George. 'Be sensible now.'

But Timmy couldn't be sensible with so many rabbits about. So they left him to chase and dart and

race at top speed and went on down the hill. Timmy
came rushing after them when they got to the bottom.

'*Now* perhaps you'll stop tearing about like a mad
thing and walk with us,' scolded George. But she
spoke too soon, for soon they were in a small wood
which Julian informed them was Coney Copse.

'And as I told you, coney means rabbit, so you
can't expect Timmy to stop being mad just yet,'
said Julian.

They very nearly lost Timmy in Coney Copse. A
rabbit disappeared down a very big hole, and Timmy
was actually able to get down a little way. Then he got
stuck. He scrabbled violently with his feet but it was
no good. He was well and truly stuck.

The others soon discovered he wasn't with them
and went back, calling. Quite by chance they came on
the hole he was in and heard the sound of panting and
scraping. A shower of sand flew out of the hole.

'There he is! The idiot, he's down a hole,' said
George in alarm. 'Timmy! TIMMY! Come on out!'

There was nothing that Timmy would have liked
better, but he couldn't come out, however much he
tried. A root of a tree had got wedged into his back,
and he couldn't seem to push himself out again, past
the annoying root.

It took the four children twenty minutes to get
Timmy out. Anne had to lie down and wriggle in a
little way to reach him. She was the only one small
enough to get into the hole.

She caught hold of Timmy's back legs and pulled
hard. Somehow the root slid off his back and he came
backwards. He whined loudly.

'Oh Anne, you're hurting him, you're hurting him!'
shouted George. 'Let him go!'

'I can't!' yelled back Anne. 'He'll only go down

deeper, if I leave go his legs. Can you pull me out? If so Timmy will come too – he'll have to because I've got his legs!'

Poor Anne was pulled out by her legs, and poor Timmy came too, pulled by his. He whined and went to George.

'He's hurt himself somewhere,' said George anxiously. 'I know he has. He wouldn't whine like that if he wasn't hurt.'

She ran her fingers over him, pressing here and there. She examined each leg and each paw. She looked at his head. Still he whined. Where could he have hurt himself?

'Leave him,' said Julian, at last. 'I can't see that he's hurt anywhere – except in his feelings! He probably didn't like Anne hauling him out by his hind legs. Most undignified!'

George wasn't satisfied. Although she could find nothing wrong, she couldn't help being sure that Timmy had hurt himself somewhere. Ought he to see a vet?

'Don't be silly, George,' said Julian. 'Vets don't grow on trees in moorland country like this! Let's go on walking. You'll see Timmy will follow quite all right, and soon forget to whine. I tell you, he's hurt his doggy feelings, that's all. His vanity is wounded!'

They left Coney Copse and went on, George rather silent. Timmy trotted beside her, also rather quiet. Still, there really didn't seem anything the matter with him, except that he gave sudden little whines now and again.

'Now here's where I thought we might have our lunch,' said Julian, at last. 'Fallaway Hill! It's a good name for it too – it falls away steeply, and we've got a marvellous view.'

So they had. They had come to the top of a steep hill, not guessing that it fell away on the other side. They could sit on the top and see the sun shining on miles and miles of lonely heather-grown moor. They might see shy deer in the distance – or little wild ponies.

'This is heavenly,' said Anne, sitting down on a great tuft of heather. 'It's as warm as summer too! I do hope it's like this all over the weekend. We shall all be burnt brown!'

'It will also be heavenly having some of those sandwiches,' said Dick, choosing a lump of heather too. 'What comfortable seats are provided for us! I've a good mind to take a tuft of this heather back to school with me to put on the very hard chair that goes with my desk!'

Julian put the four packets of sandwiches down in the heather. Anne undid them. They looked wonderful!

'Super!' said Anne. 'What do you want first?'

'Well, speaking for myself I'm going to have one of each, put them all on top of one another, and have a huge bite of cheese, ham, pork and egg at once,' said Dick. Anne laughed.

'Even *your* mouth isn't big enough for that,' she said. But somehow Dick managed, though it was difficult.

'Disgusting behaviour,' he said, when he had managed the first mouthful. 'I think on the whole that one at a time is more economical. Hie, Timmy – have a bit?'

Timmy obliged. He was very quiet, and George was still anxious about him. Still, his appetite seemed remarkably good, so nobody but George wondered any more if he had hurt himself. He lay beside George, occasionally putting a great paw on her knee if he wanted another bit of sandwich.

'Timmy does jolly well,' said Dick, with his mouth full. 'He gets bits from us all. I bet he eats more than any of us. I say – did anyone ever taste such smashing sandwiches? Have you tried the pork? It must have come from a super pig!'

It was lovely sitting there in the sun, looking over miles of countryside, eating hungrily. They all felt very happy. Except George. *Was* there anything wrong with Timmy? It would spoil the whole week-end if so!

4   George is worried

They lazed for some time in the sun after they had finished their meal. There were three sandwiches each left, and half a piece each of the fruit cake. No one had been able to manage a whole piece, much as they would have liked to.

Timmy seemed to think he could finish all the cake that was left, but Julian said no. 'It's such a gorgeous cake it would be really wasted on Timmy,' he said. 'You've had enough, Tim. Greedy dog!'

'Woof,' said Timmy, wagging his tail, and eyeing the cake watchfully. He sighed when he saw it being packed up. He had only had a bit of George's half-slice – what a cake!

'I'll pack three sandwiches and a half-slice of the cake into each of four bags,' said Julian. 'Anyone can eat his or hers whenever they like. I expect we shall have a good meal at the farmhouse I've chosen for tonight, so you can eat when you like before then.'

'I don't feel as if I could eat anything till tomorrow morning,' said Anne, putting her bag of food into her rucksack. 'But it's odd how hungry you keep on getting, even if you feel you can't possibly be for hours and hours.'

'Well, Timmy can wolf anything you don't want,' said Julian. 'Nothing wasted when Tim's about. Now are we all ready? We're going through a little village soon, where we'll stop for a drink. I could do with a ginger-beer. And then on we go to our farmhouse. We ought to try and arrive about five, because it gets dark so soon.'

'What's the farmhouse called?' asked Anne.

'Blue Pond Farm,' said Julian. 'Nice name, isn't it? I hope it's still got a blue pond.'

'Suppose they haven't room for us?' said Anne.

'Oh, they can always put a couple of girls some-where,' said Julian. 'Dick and I can sleep in a barn if necessary. We're not particular!'

'*I'd* like to sleep in a barn too,' said Anne. 'I'd love to. Let's not ask for a bedroom, let's all sleep in a barn – on straw or hay or something.'

'No,' said Julian. 'You girls will have to be in the house. It gets cold at night, and we've brought no rugs. We boys will be all right with our macs over us. I'm not letting you two girls do that.'

'It's *stupid* being a girl!' said George, for about the millionth time in her life. 'Always having to be careful when boys can do as they like! I'm going to sleep in a barn, anyway. I don't care what you say, Ju!'

'Oh yes you do,' said Julian. 'You know quite well that if ever you go against the orders of the chief – that's me, my girl, in case you didn't know it – you won't come out with us again. You may look like a boy and behave like a boy, but you're a girl all the same. And like it or not, girls have got to be taken care of.'

'I should have thought that boys hated having to take care of girls,' said George, sulkily. 'Especially girls like me who don't like it.'

'Well, decent boys like looking after their girl cousins or their sisters,' said Julian. 'And oddly enough decent girls like it. But I won't count you as a girl, George, decent or otherwise. I'll merely count you as a boy who's got to have an eye on him – my eye, see? So take that look off your face, and don't make yourself any more difficult than you already are.'

George couldn't help laughing, and the sulky look went at once. She gave Julian a punch. 'All right. You win. You're so jolly domineering these days I feel quite afraid of you!'

'You're not afraid of anyone,' said Dick. 'You're the bravest girl I ever knew! Aha! That's made old George blush like a girl! Let me warm my hands, George!'

And Dick held his hands up in front of George's scarlet face, pretending to warm them at her fiery blush. She didn't know whether to be pleased or angry. She pushed his hands away and got up, looking more like a boy than ever with her short tousled hair and her well-freckled face!

The others got up and stretched. Then they settled their rucksacks on their backs again, with their macs fastened to them, threw their blazers over their shoulders and set off down Fallaway Hill.

Timmy followed, but he didn't bound about as usual. He went slowly and carefully. George looked round for him, and frowned.

'What *is* the matter with Timmy?' she said. 'Look at him! Not a jump or a scamper in him!'

They all stopped and watched him. He came towards them and they saw that he was limping slightly with his left hind leg. George dropped down beside him and felt the leg carefully.

'I think he must have twisted it – sprained it or something, when he was down that rabbit-hole,' she said. She patted him gently on the back and he winced.

'What's the matter, Tim?' said George, and she parted the hair on his back, examining the white skin underneath to see why he had winced when she had patted him.

'He's got an awful bruise here,' she said at last, and the others bent to see. 'Something must have hurt his back down in that hole. And Anne must have hurt one of his legs when she held on to them and dragged him out. I *told* you not to hold on to his legs, Anne.'

'Well, how were we to get him out if I didn't?' demanded Anne, feeling cross but rather guilty. 'Did you want him to stick there for days and days?'

'I don't think there's much damage done,' said Julian, feeling the hind leg. 'I honestly think he's only just twisted it a bit, George. He'll be all right after tonight, I'm sure.'

'But I must be *certain*,' said George. 'Did you say we come to a village soon, Ju?'

'Yes – Beacons Village,' said Julian. 'We can ask if there's a vet anywhere in the district if you like. He'll look at Timmy's leg and tell you if there's anything much wrong. But I don't think there is.'

'We'll go on to the village then,' said George. 'Oh dear – the only time I *ever* wish Timmy was a *little* dog is when he's hurt – because he's so very very heavy to carry.'

'Well, don't think of carrying him yet,' said Dick. 'He can walk on three legs even if he can't on four! He's not as bad as all that, are you, Timmy?'

'Woof,' said Timmy, mournfully. He was rather enjoying all the fuss. George patted his head. 'Come on,' she said, 'we'll soon get that leg put right. Come on, Tim.'

They all went on, looking round to see how Timmy was getting on. He followed slowly, and then began to limp more badly. Finally he lifted his left hind leg up from the ground and ran on three legs only.

'Poor boy,' said George. 'Poor Timmy! I do hope his leg will be all right tomorrow. I can't possibly go on with the hike if it isn't.'

It was rather a gloomy company that came to Beacons Village. Julian made his way to a little inn that stood in the middle, called Three Shepherds.

A woman was shaking a duster out of a window. Julian called up to her.

'I say! Is there a vet anywhere in this district? I want someone to have a look at our dog's leg.'

'No. No vet here,' answered the woman. 'Not one nearer than Marlins over six miles away.'

George's heart sank. Timmy would never be able to walk six miles.

'Is there a bus?' she called.

'No. Not to Marlins,' said the woman. 'No bus goes there, missy. But if you want your dog's leg seen to, you go up to Spiggy House, up along there. Mr Gaston lives there with his horses, and he knows about dogs too. You take the dog there. He'll know what to do.'

'Oh *thank* you,' said George, gratefully. 'Is it very far?'

'About half a mile,' said the woman. 'See that hill?' You go up there, take the turning to the right and you'll see a big house. That's Spiggy House. You can't mistake it because of the stables built all round it. Ask for Mr Gaston. He's nice, he is. Maybe you'll have to wait a little if he's out with his horses though – he may not be in till it's almost dark.'

The four put their heads together. 'We'd better go up to this Mr Gaston's, I think,' said Julian. 'But I think you and Anne, Dick, should go on to the farm-house I planned to stay in for the night, and make arrangements for us. We don't want to leave it till the last minute. I'll go with George and Timmy, of course.'

'Right,' said Dick. 'I'll take Anne now. It will be dark pretty soon. Got your torch, Julian?'

'Yes,' said Julian. 'And I'm pretty good at finding my way, as you know. I shall come back to this village after we've been to Mr Gaston's, and then make straight for the farmhouse. It's about a mile and a half away.'

'Thanks awfully for saying you'll come with me, Julian,' said George. 'Let's go now, shall we? Well, Dick and Anne – see you later!'

Julian set off with George and Timmy up the hill to Spiggy House. Timmy went on three legs, and still seemed very sorry for himself. Anne and Dick watched him, feeling sorry for him too.

'I hope he's all right tomorrow,' said Dick. 'It will spoil our weekend if he's not, no doubt about that!'

They turned away and walked through the little village of Beacons. 'Now for Blue Pond Farmhouse,' said Dick. 'Julian didn't give me very clear directions. I think I'll ask someone exactly where it is.'

But they met nobody except a man driving a little cart. Dick hailed him and he pulled up his horse.

'Are we on the right road for Blue Pond Farmhouse?' shouted Dick.

'Ar,' answered the man, nodding his head.

'Is it straight on – or do we take any paths or little lanes?' asked Dick.

'Ar,' said the man, nodding again.

'What does he mean – "ar"?' said Dick. He raised his voice again.

'Is it this way?' and he pointed.

'Ar,' said the man again. He raised his whip and

pointed up the road where the two were going, and then across to the west.

'Oh, I see – we turn to the right up there?' called Dick.

'Ar,' said the man, nodding, and drove on so suddenly that the horse almost stepped on Dick's foot.

'Well – if we find the farmhouse after all those "ars" we'll be clever,' said Dick. 'Come on!'

5 Anne and Dick

It began to get dark very suddenly. The sun had gone,
and a big black cloud slid smoothly over the sky. 'It's
going to rain,' said Dick. 'Blow! I thought it was
going to be a lovely evening.'

'We'd better hurry,' said Anne. 'I hate sheltering
under a hedge in the pouring rain, with drips down my
neck, and puddles round my feet!'

They hurried. They went up the road that led out of
the village and then came to a turning on the right.
This must be the one the man had meant. They
stopped and looked down it. It seemed to be like one of
the sunken lanes they had walked down in the morning, and it looked rather dark and tunnel-like now, in
the twilight.

'I hope it's right,' said Dick. 'We'll ask the very first
person we meet.'

'If we *do* meet anyone!' said Anne, feeling that they
never would in this curious deep lane. They went up
it. It wound round and about and then went downhill
into a very muddy bit indeed. Anne found herself
sloshing about in thick mud.

'A stream or something must run across the lane
here,' she said. 'Ugh! The water's got into my shoes!
I'm sure we don't go this way, Dick. The water's quite
deep farther on, I'm certain. I was up to my ankles just
now.'

Dick looked about in the deepening twilight. He

made out something above him in the high hedge that grew on the steep bank each side.

'Look – is that a stile?' he said, 'Where's my torch? At the bottom of my rucksack, of course! Can you get it out, Anne, to save me taking the thing off?'

Anne found the torch and gave it to Dick. He switched it on, and immediately the shadows round them grew blacker, and the lane seemed more tunnel-like than ever. Dick flashed the torch upwards to what he had thought was a stile.

'Yes – it is a stile,' he said. 'I expect that leads up to the farmhouse – a short cut, probably. I've no doubt this lane is the one used by the farm-carts, and probably goes right round to the farm – but if this is a short cut we might as well take it. It must lead somewhere, anyway!'

They scrambled up the bank to the stile. Dick helped Anne over, and they found themselves in a wide field. In front of them was a narrow path, running between crops of some sort.

'Yes – this is obviously a short cut,' said Dick, pleased. 'I expect we'll see the lights of the farmhouse in a minute.'

'Or fall into the blue pond first,' said Anne, rather dismally. It was just beginning to rain and she was wondering if it was worth while to untie her mac from her shoulder and put it on. Or was the farmhouse really nearby? Julian had said it wasn't very far.

They walked across the field and came to another stile. The rain was coming down fast now. Anne decided to put on her mac. She stood under a thick bush and Dick helped her on with it. She had a small sou'wester in the pocket and put that on too. Dick put his on and they set off again.

The second stile led into another endless field, and

the path then came at last to a big field-gate. They climbed over it and found themselves on what looked like a heathery moor – wild and uncultivated land! No farmhouse was to be seen – though, indeed, they could not have seen anything of one unless they had been very close to it, because the night was on them, dark and rainy.

'If only we could see lights somewhere – shining out of a window,' said Dick. He shone his torch on to the moor in front of them. 'I don't quite know what to do. There doesn't seem to be a path here – and I just hate the idea of going all the way back across those wet fields, and into that dark little lane.'

'Oh no – don't let's,' said Anne, with a shiver. 'I really didn't like that lane. There *must* be a path somewhere! It's silly for a gate to open on to moorland!'

And then, as they stood there, with the rain dripping on them and not much else to be heard, another noise came to their ears.

It was so unexpected and so very startling that both of them clutched the other in a start of alarm. It was certainly a strange noise to hear in that deserted bit of country.

Bells! Wild, clanging bells sounding without a stop, jangling out over the dark countryside in peal after peal. Anne held on tightly to Dick.

'What is it? Where are those bells? What are they ringing for?' whispered Anne.

Dick had no idea. He was as startled as Anne to hear this extraordinary noise. It sounded some distance away, but every now and again the wind blew hard and then the noise of the jangling swept round them, close to them it seemed.

'I wish they'd stop. Oh, I wish they'd stop!' said

Anne, her heart, beating fast. 'I don't like them. They frighten me. They're not church bells.'

'No. They're certainly not church bells,' said Dick. 'They're a warning of some kind. I'm sure – but what for? Fire? We'd see fire if there was one anywhere near us. War? No – bells and beacons were used to warn people of war long long ago. Not now.'

'That village was called Beacons,' said Anne, suddenly remembering. 'Do you suppose it has that name because long ago there was a nearby hill where people lighted a beacon, to send a warning to other towns telling them that the enemy was coming? Did they ring bells too? Are we hearing long-ago bells, Dick? They don't sound like bells I've ever heard in my life before.'

'Good gracious! They're certainly not long-ago bells!' said Dick, speaking cheerfully, though he was really just as puzzled and alarmed as Anne. 'Those bells are being rung now, at this very minute!'

Quite suddenly the bells stopped and an enormous silence took the place of the wild ringing. The two children stood and listened for a minute or two and then heaved a sigh of relief.

'They've stopped at last,' said Anne. 'I hated them! *Why* did they ring out on this dark dark night? Oh do let's find Blue Pond Farmhouse as soon as ever we can, Dick. I don't like being lost in the dark like this, with bells ringing madly for nothing at all!'

'Come on,' said Dick. 'Keep close to the hedge. As long as we follow that we must come to somewhere. We won't wander out on to the moorland.'

He took Anne's arm and the two of them kept close to the hedge. They came to another path at last and followed it. That led to a lane, but not a sunken one this time – and then, oh wonderful sight – not far off they saw a light shining!

'That must be Blue Pond Farmhouse!' said Dick, thankfully. 'Come on, Anne – not much farther now!'

They came to a low stone wall and followed it till they came to a broken-down gate. It opened with a squeak, and Anne stepped through – right into an enormous puddle!

'Blow!' she said. 'Now I'm wetter than ever! For a moment I thought I must have stepped into the blue pond!'

But it was only a puddle. They went round it and followed a muddy path to a little door set in a white stone wall. Dick thought it must be the back door. Nearby was a window, and in it shone the light they had seen so thankfully.

An old woman sat near the light, her head bent over some sewing. The children could see her quite clearly as they stood by the door.

Dick looked for a bell or knocker but there was none. He knocked with his bare knuckles. Nobody answered. The door remained shut. They looked at the old woman by the lamp, and saw that she was still sewing.

'Perhaps she's deaf,' said Dick and he knocked again, much more loudly. Still the old woman sewed on placidly. She must indeed be deaf!

'We'll never get in at this rate!' said Dick, impatiently. He tried the handle of the door – it opened at once!

'We'll just have to walk in and announce ourselves,' said Dick, and he stepped on to the worn mat inside the door. He was in a narrow little passage that led to a stone stairway, steep and narrow at the farther end.

On his right was a door, a little ajar. It opened into

the room where the old woman was sitting. The two children could see a streak of light coming through the crack.

Dick pushed the door open and walked boldly in, followed by Anne. Still the old woman didn't look up. She pushed her needle in and out of her sewing and seemed to hear and see nothing else whatsoever.

Dick had to walk right up to her before she knew he was in the room. Then she leapt up in such a fright that her chair fell over with a bang.

'I'm sorry,' said Dick, upset at frightening the old lady. 'We knocked but you didn't hear!'

She stared at them, her hand over her heart. 'You give me such a fright,' she said. 'Where did you come from this dark night?'

Dick picked up her chair, and she sat down in it, panting a little.

'We've been looking for this place,' said Dick. 'Blue Pond Farmhouse, isn't it? We wondered if we could stay the night here – and two others of us as well.'

The old woman pointed to her ears and shook her head. 'Deaf as a post,' she said. 'No good talking to me, my dear. You've lost your way, I suppose?'

Dick nodded.

'Well, you can't stay here,' said the old woman. 'My son won't have no one here at all. You'd best be gone before he comes. He have a nasty temper, he have.'

Dick shook his head. Then he pointed out to the dark rainy night, then pointed to Anne's wet shoes and clothes. The old woman knew what he meant.

'You've lost your way, you're wet and tired, and you don't want me to turn you out,' she said. 'But there's my son, you see. He don't like strangers here.'

Dick pointed to Anne, and then to a sofa in a corner of the room. Then he pointed to himself, and then outside. Again the old woman understood at once.

'You want me to give your sister shelter, but you'll go out into the night?' she said. Dick nodded. He thought he could easily find some shed or barn for himself. But Anne really must be indoors.

'My son mustn't see either of you,' said the old woman, and she pulled Anne to what the girl thought was a cupboard. But when the door opened, she saw a very small, steep wooden staircase leading upwards into the roof.

'You go up there,' said the old woman to Anne. 'And don't you come down till I call you in the morning. I'll get into trouble if my son knows you're here.'

'Go up, Anne,' said Dick, rather troubled. 'I don't know what you'll find there. If it's too bad, come down. See if there's a window or something you can call out from, and then I'll know if you're all right.'

'Yes,' said Anne, in rather a trembling voice, and she went up the steep, dirty wooden stairs. They led straight into a little loft. There was a mattress there, fairly clean, and a chair. A rug was folded up on the chair and a jug of water stood on a shelf. Otherwise the room was bare.

A tiny window opened out on one side. Anne went to it and called out. 'Dick! Are you there? Dick!'

'Yes, I'm here,' said Dick. 'What's it like, Anne? Is it all right? Listen, I'll find somewhere nearby to shelter in – and you can always call me if you want me!'

6 *In the middle of the night*

'It's not bad,' said Anne. 'There's a fairly clean mattress and a rug. I'll be all right. But what about if the others come, Dick? Will you look out for them? I almost think George will have to sleep in a barn with you and Julian if she comes. That old woman won't let anyone else in, I'm sure!'

'I'll look out for them and arrange something,' said Dick. 'You eat the rest of your sandwiches and your cake, and see if you can dry your wet feet and make yourself really comfortable. There's a shed or something out here. I shall be quite all right. Yell for me if you want me.'

Anne went back into the room. She felt wet and tired, hungry and thirsty. She ate all her food, and had a drink from the jug. Then she felt sleepy and lay down on the mattress, throwing the rug over her. She meant to listen for the others to come, but she was too tired. She fell fast asleep!

Dick was prowling about down below. He was careful because he didn't want to run into the old woman's son. He didn't like the sound of him somehow! He came to a small barn with piles of straw in one corner. He flashed his torch cautiously round.

'This will do for me,' he thought. 'I can be quite comfortable here in that straw. Poor Anne! I wish old George was with her. I'd better wait about and watch for the other two, or I'll fall asleep and miss them, once

I bed down in that straw! It's only about six o'clock too – but we've had a long day. I wonder how Timmy is. I wish he was here!'

Dick thought that probably George and Julian would come in through the same gate as he and Anne had used. He found a broken-down shed near the gate and sat down on a box there, waiting for them to come.

He ate his sandwiches while he waited. They were very comforting! He ate every one and then the cake. He yawned. He felt very sleepy indeed, and his feet were wet and tired.

No one arrived at all – not even the old woman's son. She could still be seen sewing under the lamp. But after about two hours, when it was almost eight o'clock, and Dick was beginning to be very worried about George and Julian, the old woman got up and put away her work-basket.

She disappeared out of Dick's sight, and didn't come back. But the light was still there, shining out of the window. Left for her son, probably, thought Dick.

He tiptoed to the window. The rain had stopped now and the night was much clearer. The stars were out and a moon was coming up. Dick's spirits rose.

He peered in at the lighted room. Then he saw the old woman lying on a broken-down sofa in a corner. A blanket was pulled right up to her chin and she seemed to be asleep. Dick went back to his shed, but now he felt there was no use in watching for George and Julian. They must have lost their way completely! Or else Mr Gaston, or whatever his name was, must have had to do something to Timmy's leg, and Julian had decided to stay at the inn in Beacons Village for the night.

He yawned again. 'I'm too sleepy to watch any more,' he decided. 'I shall fall off this box with sleep if I don't go and lie down in that straw. Anyway I think I'd hear if the others came.'

Using his torch cautiously, he made his way to the barn. He shut the door behind him and bolted it roughly from the inside by running a stick through two hasps. He didn't know why he did that – perhaps because he was still thinking of the old woman's bad-tempered son!

He flung himself down on the straw, and immediately fell asleep. Outside the sky became clearer and clearer. The moon came up, not fully, but large enough to give some light. It shone down on the desolate little stone house and ill-kept outbuildings.

Dick slept soundly. He lay in the soft straw and dreamed of Timmy and George and Blue Ponds and bells. Especially bells.

He awoke suddenly, and lay for a moment wondering where he was. What was this prickly stuff round him? Then he remembered – of course, it was straw and he was in a barn! He was about to cuddle down again when he heard a noise.

It was only a small noise – a scratching on the wooden walls of the barn perhaps. Dick sat up. Were there rats there? He hoped not!

He listened. The scratching seemed to come from *outside* the barn, not inside. Then it stopped. After an interval it began again. Then there came a gentle tapping at the broken window just above Dick's head.

He felt very startled. Rats scratched and scrabbled about – but they didn't tap on windows. Who was tapping so very cautiously on the little window? He held his breath and listened, straining his ears.

And then he heard a voice – a hoarse whisper.

'Dick! Dick!'

Dick was amazed. Could it be Julian? If so, how in the world did he know that he, Dick, was in the barn? He sat listening, stiff with surprise.

The tapping came again, and then the voice, a little louder. 'Dick! I know you're there. I saw you go in. Come here to the window – quiet, now!'

Dick didn't know the voice. It wasn't Julian's, and it certainly wasn't either George's or Anne's. Then how did the owner know *his* name and that he was there? It was astounding. Dick didn't know what to do!

'Buck up!' said the voice. 'I've got to go in half a tick. I've got that message for you.'

Dick decided to go nearer to the window. He was quite certain that he didn't want whoever it was outside to come into the barn. He cautiously knelt up in the straw and spoke just underneath the window.

'I'm here,' he said, trying to make his voice deep and grown-up.

'You've been long enough coming,' grumbled the one outside, and then Dick saw him through the window – just a face, dim and wild-eyed, with a round bullet-like head. He crouched back, thankful that the face couldn't see him in the darkness of the barn.

'Here's the message from Nailer,' said the voice. 'Two-Trees. Gloomy Water. Saucy Jane. And he says Maggie knows. He sent you this. Maggie's got one too.'

A bit of paper fluttered in at the broken pane. Dick picked it up in a daze. What *was* all this? Was he dreaming?

The voice came again, insistent and urgent. 'You heard all that, Dick? Two-Trees. Gloomy Water. Saucy Jane. And Maggie knows too. Now I'm going.'

There came the sound of someone cautiously creep-

ing round the barn – and then there was silence. Dick
sat amazed and bewildered. Who was this wild-eyed
fellow, who called him by his name in the middle of
the night and gave him extraordinary messages that
meant nothing at all to a sleepy boy? But Dick was
wide awake now. He stood up and looked out of the
window. There was nothing and no one to be seen
except the lonely house and the sky.

Dick sat down again and thought. He put his torch
on cautiously and looked at the piece of paper he had
picked up. It was a dirty half sheet, with pencil marks
on it that meant nothing to Dick at all. Words were
printed here and there, but they were all nonsense to
him. He simply couldn't make head or tail of his
visitor, his message or the bit of paper!

'I'm sure I must be dreaming,' thought Dick, and
put the paper into his pocket. He lay back in his straw,
cuddling in deep, because he had got cold by the
window. He lay and thought for a while, puzzling
over the curious happenings, and then he felt his eyes
closing.

But before he was quite asleep, he heard cautious
footsteps again! Was that fellow back once more? This
time someone tried the door – but the wooden stick
was in the hasps. Whoever it was outside shook the
door and the stick fell out at once. The man shook the
door again as if thinking it had stuck, and then opened
it. He came inside and shut the door behind him.

Dick caught a quick glimpse of him. No – this
wasn't the same man as before. This was a man with a
head of thick hair. Dick hoped and prayed that he
wouldn't come over to the straw.

He didn't. He sat down on a sack and waited. He
talked to himself after a while, but Dick could only
make out a word or two.

'What's happpened?' he heard. 'How much longer do I wait?' Then there was a mumble and Dick could not catch a word.

'Wait, wait – that's all I do,' muttered the man, and he stood up and stretched himself. Then he went to the door and looked out. He came back and sat down on the sack again.

He sat still and quiet then, and Dick found his eyes closing once more. Was this part of a dream too? He didn't have time to think it out because he was suddenly in a real dream, walking along ringing bells and seeing trees in twos everywhere round him!

He slept heavily all night long. When morning came he awoke suddenly and sat up. He was alone in the barn. Where had the second visitor gone? Or *could* it all have been a dream?

7 In the morning

Dick stood up and stretched himself. He felt dirty and untidy. Also he was very hungry. He wondered if the old woman would let him buy some bread and cheese and a glass of milk.

'Anne must be hungry too,' he thought. 'I wonder if she's all right.' He went cautiously outside and looked up at the tiny window of the loft where Anne had spent the night. Her anxious face was already there, watching for Dick!

'Are you all right, Anne?' called Dick, in a low tone. She pushed open the tiny window and smiled at him.

'Yes. But I daren't go down because that son is downstairs. I can hear him shouting at the deaf old woman every now and again. He sounds very bad-tempered.'

'I'll wait for him to go out to his work then, before I go and see the old woman,' said Dick. 'I must pay her something for letting you sleep up in that loft — and perhaps I can persuade her to let us have something to eat.'

'I wish you could,' said Anne. 'I've eaten all the chocolate I had in my bag. Shall I wait till I hear you call me?'

Dick nodded and disappeared into the barn in a hurry. He had heard footsteps!

A man came into sight — a broad, short, hunched-up man, with a shock of untidy hair. He was the man that

Dick had seen in the barn the night before. He was muttering to himself and looked very bad-tempered indeed. Dick decided to keep out of his way. He crouched down in the barn.

But the man did not go in there. He walked past, still muttering. Dick listened for his footsteps to die away. He heard the opening of a gate somewhere, then it crashed behind the man.

'I'd better take my chance now,' thought Dick, and he went quickly out of the barn and up to the little white house. It looked very tumble-down and neglected in the daylight, and had a more forlorn air.

Dick knew that it was no good knocking, because the old woman wouldn't hear him. So he walked right into the house and found the woman washing up a few dishes in a cracked old sink. She stared at him in dismay.

'I'd forgotten about you! And the girl too! Is she still up there? Get her down quickly before my son comes back! And then go, both of you!'

'Can you sell us some bread and cheese?' shouted Dick. But the old woman really was stone deaf, and all she did was to push Dick away towards the door, jabbing at him with the wet cloth in her hand. Dick slipped aside and pointed to some bread on a table.

'No, no – I tell you, you're to go,' said the old woman, obviously terrified in case her son should come back. 'Get the girl, quickly!'

But before Dick could do anything, there were footsteps outside and in came the hunched-up fellow with the shock of hair! He was back already, holding some eggs he had been to find.

He walked into the kitchen and stared at Dick. 'Clear out!' he said, angrily. 'What do you want here?'

Dick thought he had better not say he had slept the

night in the barn. There were strange goings-on here, and the man might be very savage if he knew Dick had slept the night nearby.

'I wanted to know if your mother could sell us some bread,' he said, and could have bitten his tongue out. He had said 'us'! Now the man would guess there was someone with him.

'Us? Who's "us"?' said the man, looking round. 'You fetch him and I'll tell you both what I do to boys who come stealing my eggs!'

'I'll go and fetch him,' said Dick, seizing the chance to get away. He ran to the door. The man made a clumsy dart at him and almost caught him. But Dick was out and away, running down the path. He hid behind a shed, his heart thumping. He had to wait for Anne. Somehow he had to go back and get her.

The man stood at the door, shouting angrily after Dick. But he didn't chase him. He went back into the house and after a while came out again with a pail of steaming food. Dick guessed he was going to feed the chickens wherever they were.

He had to take this chance of fetching Anne. He waited till he heard the crash of the distant gate again and then he rushed to the house. Anne's face was at the window, scared. She had heard all that the man had said to Dick, and then to his mother about allowing boys to come to the house.

'Anne! Come down at once. He's gone,' shouted Dick. 'Hurry!'

Anne's face disappeared from the window. She ran to the door, tumbled quickly down the stairs, and ran through the kitchen. The old woman flapped a cloth at her, screaming at her.

Dick ran into the kitchen and put a pound coin on the table. Then he caught Anne's arm and both children tore out of the house and down the path. They came to the hedge they had followed the night before.

Anne was quite scared. 'That awful man!' she said. 'Oh Dick – what a horrible place. Honestly I think Julian must be mad to choose a place like that to sleep in for the night – horrible little house! And it didn't look a bit like a farm. There were no cows or pigs that I could see and not even a farm-dog!'

'You know, Anne, I don't think it could possibly have been Blue Pond Farmhouse,' said Dick, as they walked beside the hedge, looking for the gate that they had come through the night before. 'We made a mistake. It was an ordinary cottage. If we hadn't lost our way we'd have come to the proper Blue Pond Farmhouse I'm sure.'

'Whatever will George and Julian be thinking?' said Anne. 'They'll be dreadfully worried, won't they, wondering what has become of us? Do you suppose they're at the real Blue Pond Farmhouse?'

'We'll have to find out,' said Dick. 'Do I look very messy and untidy, Anne? I feel awful.'

'Yes. Haven't you a comb?' said Anne. 'Your hair's all up on end. And your face is very dirty. Look, there's a little stream over there. Let's get our flannels out and wash our hands and faces with them.'

They did a little washing in the cold water of the stream, and Dick combed back his hair.

'You look a lot better,' said Anne. 'Oh dear – I wish we could have some breakfast. I'm really starving! I didn't sleep awfully well, did you, Dick? My mattress was so hard, and I was rather scared, up in that funny little room all alone.'

Before Dick could answer, a boy came whistling

through the gate. He looked astonished to see Dick and Anne.

'Hallo!' he said. 'You hiking?'

'Yes,' said Dick. 'Can you tell me if that place up there is Blue Pond Farmhouse?'

He pointed back to the old woman's house. The boy laughed.

'That's no farmhouse. That's Mrs Taggart's place, and a dirty old place it is. Don't you go there, or her son will drive you off. Dirty Dick we call him – he's a terror! Blue Pond Farmhouse is down along there, see? Past the Three Shepherds Inn and away up to the left.'

'Thanks,' said Dick, feeling very angry indeed with the man who had said 'ar' and sent them all wrong the day before. The boy waved, and set off across a moorland path.

'We certainly went the wrong way last night,' said Dick, as they walked over the fields they had crossed in the dark the night before. 'Poor Anne! Dragging you all that way in the dark and the rain to a horrible place that wasn't Blue Pond Farmhouse after all. I can't think what Julian is going to say to me.'

'Well, it was my fault too,' said Anne. 'Dick, let's go down to the Three Shepherds and telephone Blue Pond Farmhouse from there, shall we? If it's on the phone, that is. I don't somehow feel as if I want to walk for miles and perhaps not find Blue Pond Farmhouse again.'

'Good idea,' said Dick. 'The Three Shepherds was where that woman was shaking a duster out of the window, wasn't it? She told Julian the way to Spiggy House. I wonder how old Timmy is. I hope he's better. I say – this hike isn't as good as we hoped it would be, is it?'

'Well, there's still time for it to be all right!' said Anne, much more cheerfully than she felt. She so badly wanted her breakfast that she felt quite bad-tempered!

'We'll telephone to Julian from the Three Shepherds to say what happened to us,' said Dick, as they came to the lane where they had floundered in the mud the night before. He helped Anne over the stile and they jumped down to the narrow road. 'And what's more, we'll have breakfast at the Three Shepherds – and I bet we eat more than ever the Three Shepherds did, whoever they were!'

Anne felt more cheerful at once. She had thought they would have to walk all the way to find Blue Pond Farmhouse before they had breakfast!

'See – a stream does flow right across the road here,' she said. 'No wonder I got my feet wet yesterday! Come on – the thought of breakfast makes my legs want to run!'

They at last arrived in Beacons Village, and made their way to the inn. On the sign three shepherds were painted, looking rather gloomy.

'They look like I feel,' said Anne, 'but I shall soon feel different. Oh Dick – think of porridge – and bacon and eggs – and toast and marmalade!'

'We must telephone first,' said Dick, firmly – and then he suddenly stopped, just as he was going into the inn. Someone was calling him.

'DICK! DICK! ANNE! Look, there they are! Hey, Dick, DICK!'

It was Julian's voice! Dick swung round in delight. He saw Julian, George and Timmy racing along the village street, shouting and waving. Timmy was first to reach them of course – and there was no sign of limping either! He leapt on them, barking madly, and licked every bare part of them he could reach.

'Oh, Ju! I'm so glad to see you!' said Anne, in rather a trembling voice. 'We lost our way last night. George, is Timmy all right?'

'Quite. Absolutely,' said George. 'You see . . .'

'Have you had breakfast? interrupted Julian. 'We haven't. We were so worried about you we were just going to see the police. But now we can all have breakfast together and tell our news!'

8   *All together again*

It was wonderful to be all together again. Julian took hold of Anne's arm and squeezed it. 'All right, Anne?' he said, rather worried at her pale face.

Anne nodded. She felt better at once, now she had Julian, George and Timmy, as well as Dick. 'I'm only just terribly hungry,' she said.

'I'll ask for breakfast straight away,' said Julian. 'All news later!'

The woman who had leaned out of the window shaking a duster the evening before, came up to them. 'I expect it's a bit late for you,' said Julian. 'But we haven't had any breakfast. What have you got?'

'Porridge and cream,' said the woman. 'And our own cured bacon and our own eggs. Our own honey and the bread I bake myself. Will that do? And coffee with cream?'

'I could hug you,' said Julian, beaming at her. The others felt the same. They went into a small, cosy dining-room and sat down to wait. Soon a smell of frying bacon and hot strong coffee would come into the room – what joy!

'Your news first,' said Dick, patting Timmy. 'Did you get to Spiggy House? Was Mr Gaston there?'

'No, he wasn't,' said Julian. 'He was out some-where. He had a very nice wife who made us wait for him, and said he wouldn't mind in the least looking at

Timmy when he came back. So we waited and waited.'

'We waited till half past seven!' said George, 'and we felt rather awkward because we thought it might be getting near their meal-time. And then at last Mr Gaston came.'

'He was awfully kind,' said Julian. 'He looked at Timmy's leg, and then he did something, I don't know what – put it back into place, I suppose – and Timmy gave a yell and George flung herself on him, and Mr Gaston roared with laughter at George . . .'

'Well, he was very *rough* with Timmy's leg,' said George. 'But he knew what he was doing, of course, and now Timmy is perfectly all right, except for that bruise on his back, and even that is getting better. He can run as well as ever.'

'I'm glad,' said Anne. 'I kept thinking of poor old Tim all last night.' She patted him, and he licked her lavishly and wetly.

'What did you do then?' asked Dick.

'Well, Mrs Gaston insisted on us staying to supper,' said Julian. 'She simply wouldn't take no for an answer, and I must say that by that time we were jolly hungry. So we stayed – and we had a jolly good meal too. So did Timmy! You should have seen his tummy afterwards – as round as a barrel. Good thing it's gone down today or I was thinking of changing his name to Tummy.' They all laughed, George especially.

'Idiot,' she said. 'Well, we didn't leave till about nine o'clock. We didn't worry about you because we felt sure you would be safely at Blue Pond Farmhouse and would guess we'd had to wait about with Timmy. And when we got there and found you hadn't arrived – well, we *were* in a state!'

'And then we thought you must have found

somewhere else for the night,' said Julian, 'but we thought if we heard nothing we'd go down to the police first thing this morning and report your disappearance!'

'So down we came – without any breakfast either!' said George. 'That shows how worried we were! Blue Pond Farmhouse was nice. They gave us a bed each in two tiny little rooms, and Timmy slept with me, of course.'

A wonderful smell came creeping into the little dining-room, followed by the inn-woman carrying a large tray. On it was a steaming tureen of porridge, a bowl of golden syrup, a jug of very thick cream, and a dish of bacon and eggs, all piled high on crisp brown toast. Little mushrooms were on the same dish.

'It's like magic!' and Anne, staring. 'Just the very things I longed for!'

'Toast, marmalade and butter to come, and the coffee and hot milk,' said the woman, busily setting everything out. 'And if you want any more bacon and eggs, just ring the bell.'

'Too good to be true!' said Dick, looking at the table. 'For goodness' sake, help yourselves quickly, girls, or I shall forget my manners and grab.'

It was a wonderful breakfast – extra wonderful because they were all so ravenously hungry. There wasn't a word said as they spooned up their porridge and cream, sweetened with golden syrup. Timmy had a dishful too – he loved porridge, though he didn't like the syrup – it made his whiskers sticky!

'I feel better,' said Anne, looking at the porridge dish. 'The thing is – shall I have some more porridge and risk not enjoying my bacon and eggs so much – or shall I go straight on with bacon and eggs?'

'A difficult question,' said Dick. 'And one that I am

faced with too. On the whole I think I'll go on with bacon and eggs – we can always have more of those if we want to – and those little mushrooms really do make my mouth water! Aren't we greedy? But how can anyone help that when they're so hungry?'

'You haven't told us a single word of what happened to *you* last night,' said Julian, serving out the bacon and eggs with a generous hand. 'Now that you've got something inside you, perhaps you feel able to tell us exactly why you ignored my instructions and didn't arrive where you were supposed to last night.'

'You sound like our headmaster at school!' said Dick. 'The plain fact is – we got lost! And when we did finally arrive somewhere, we thought it was Blue Pond Farmhouse, and we stayed the night there.'

'I see,' said Julian. 'But didn't the people there tell you it wasn't the right place? Just so that you could have let us know? You must have known that we would worry about you.'

'Well, the old woman there was stone-deaf,' explained Anne, attacking her bacon and eggs vigorously. 'She didn't understand a word we said, and as we thought it *was* Blue Pond Farmhouse, we stayed there – though it was a horrible place. And *we* were worried because *you* didn't arrive!'

'A chapter of accidents,' said Julian. 'All's well that ends well, however.'

'Don't sound so pompous!' said Dick. 'Actually we had a pretty poor time, Ju. Poor Anne had to sleep in a little loft, and I slept in straw in a barn – not that I minded that – but – well, peculiar things happened in the night. At least – I *think* they did. I'm not really sure it wasn't all a dream.'

'What peculiar things?' asked Julian at once.

'Well – I think perhaps I'll tell you when we're on our way again,' said Dick. 'Now I think about it in full daylight I feel that either it was all a silly dream – or – well, as I said – something very peculiar.'

'You never told me, Dick!' said Anne, in surprise.

'Well, to tell you the truth I forgot about it because other things happened,' said Dick. 'Having to get away from that man, for instance – and wondering about Julian and George – and feeling so hungry.'

'You don't sound as if you had a good night at all,' said George. 'It must have been awful, too, trying to find your way in the dark. It poured with rain, didn't it?'

'Yes,' said Anne, 'but oh – the thing that frightened me more than anything was the bells! Did you hear them Julian? They suddenly clanged out, and they made me terribly scared. I couldn't think what they were! Whatever were they ringing out for? They were so loud.'

'Didn't you know what they were ringing for?' said Julian. 'They were bells rung from the prison that nice old woman told us about – they were rung to tell everyone in the countryside that a prisoner had escaped! Lock your doors. Guard your folk.'

Anne stared at Julian in silence. So that was why the bells had made such a clamour and clangour. She shivered.

'I'm glad I didn't know that,' she said. 'I would have slept in the straw with Dick if I'd known there was an escaped prisoner. Have they caught him?'

'I don't know,' said Julian. 'We'll ask the inn-woman when she comes.'

They asked her, and she shook her head. 'No. He's not caught yet. But he will be. All the roads from the moor are guarded and everyone is on the watch. He was a robber who broke into houses and attacked anyone who tried to prevent him. A dangerous fellow.'

'Julian – is it all right to go hiking on the moors if there's an escaped prisoner about?' said Anne. 'I shan't feel very comfortable.'

'We've got Timmy,' said Julian. 'He would be strong enough to protect us from three prisoners if necessary! You needn't worry.'

'Woof,' agreed Timmy, at once, and thumped his tail on the floor.

At last everyone had finished breakfast. Even starving Anne couldn't manage the last bit of toast. She sighed happily. 'I feel myself again,' she announced. 'I can't say I feel very much like walking – but I know it would be good for me after that enormous meal.'

'Good or not, we're going on our way,' said Julian, getting up. 'I'll buy some sandwiches first.'

The inn-woman was delighted with their hearty praises. She gave them some packets of sandwiches and waved good-bye. 'You come again whenever you can,' she said. 'I'll always have something nice for you.'

The four went down the street and took a lane at the bottom. It wound about for a short way and then came into a valley. A stream ran down the middle of the valley. The children could hear it gurgling from where they stood.

'Lovely!' said Anne. 'Are we going along by the stream? I'd like to.'

Julian looked at his map. 'Yes – we could,' he said. 'I've marked the path to follow, and the stream joins it some way on. So if you like we could go along by it, though it will be very rough walking.'

They made their way to the stream. 'Now Dick,'

said Julian, when they had left the path. 'What about telling us all those peculiar things that happened in the night? There's nobody about to hear – not a soul in sight. Let's hear everything. We'll soon tell you whether it was a dream or not.'

'Right,' said Dick. 'Well, here's the tale. It does sound pretty peculiar. Listen . . .'

9 Dick surprises the others

Dick began his tale – but it was really very difficult to hear it because they couldn't walk four abreast, as there was no path to follow.

In the end Julian stopped and pointed to a thick clump of heather. 'Let's go and sit there and hear Dick's story properly. I keep missing bits. No one can hear us if we sit here.'

They sat down and Dick started again. He told about the old woman who was afraid her son would be angry if she let them stay the night. He told about his bed in the straw.

'And now here comes the bit I think must have been a dream,' he said. 'I woke up to hear a scratching noise on the wooden walls of the barn . . .'

'Rats or mice?' said George, and Timmy leapt up at once, of course. He was sure she had said the words to him!

'I thought that too,' said Dick. 'But then I heard a gentle tap-tap-tapping on the window.'

'How horrid,' said Anne. 'I shouldn't have liked that at all.'

'Neither did I,' said Dick. 'But the *next* thing I heard was my name being called!' "Dick! Dick!" Just like that.'

'It *must* have been a dream then,' said Anne. 'There was no one there who knew your name.'

Dick went on. 'Well, then the voice said – "Dick! I

know you're there. I saw you go in!" And it told me to go to the window.'

'Go on,' said Julian. He was puzzled. No one in the world but Anne could have known that Dick was in the barn – and it certainly wasn't Anne out there in the night!

'Well, I went to the window,' said Dick, 'and I saw, rather dimly, of course, a wild-eyed looking fellow. He couldn't see me in the darkness of the barn. I just mumbled, "I'm here," hoping he would think I was whoever he wanted.'

'What did he say next?' said George.

'He said something that sounded stuff and non-sense,' said Dick. 'He said it twice. It was "Two-Trees. Gloomy Water. Saucy Jane." And he said "Maggie knows." Just like that!'

There was silence. Then George laughed. 'Two-Trees! Gloomy Water! Saucy Jane – and Maggie knows about it! Well, it *must* have been a dream, Dick! You know it must. What do you think, Julian?'

'Well – it does sound a bit nonsensical to have someone come in the middle of the night and call Dick by name and give him a strange message that doesn't mean a thing to him!' said Julian. 'It sounds more dream-like than real. I'd say it was a dream too.'

Dick began to think they were right – and then a sudden thought struck him. He sat up straight. 'Wait a bit!' he said. 'I've remembered something! The man slipped a bit of paper through the broken pane of the window, and I picked it up!'

'Ah – that's different,' said Julian. 'Now – if you can't find that paper, it's all a dream and you dreamt the paper too – but if you *can* find it, well the whole thing is true. Very peculiar indeed – but true.'

Dick searched quickly in his pockets. He felt paper

in one of them, and drew it out. It was a dirty, crumpled piece, with a few words on it and a few lines. He held it out to the others in silence, his eyes shining.

'Is this the paper?' asked Julian. 'My word – so you didn't dream it after all, then!'

He took the paper. Four heads bent over it to examine it. No, five – because Timmy wanted to see what they were all so interested in. He thrust his hairy head between Julian's and Dick's.

'I can't make any sense of this paper,' said Julian. 'It's a plan of some kind, I think – but what of, or where, it's impossible to know.'

'The fellow said that Maggie had one of these bits of paper too,' said Dick, remembering.

'Who in the wide world *is* Maggie?' said George, 'and why should Maggie know?'

'Any more to tell?' asked Julian, intensely interested now.

'Well – the son of the deaf old woman came into the barn later on,' said Dick. 'And he sat and waited and waited, and muttered and muttered – and then when I woke up he wasn't there. So I thought I must have dreamt him too. He didn't see me, of course.'

Julian pursed up his lips and frowned. Then Anne spoke excitedly.

'Dick! Ju! I think I know why the second man came into the barn. It was the *second* man that the wild-eyed man wanted to give the message to, and the bit of paper – not to Dick. He didn't want *Dick*. But he had seen him creep into the barn, and I suppose he thought Dick was the man he really wanted and that he was in the barn waiting for him!'

'That's all very well – but how did he know my name?' asked Dick.

'He didn't know it! He didn't know it was you at

all!' said Anne, excitedly. 'The other man's name must have been Dick too! Don't you *see*? They must have planned to meet there, the wild-eyed man and the old woman's son – and the first man saw Dick go in, so he waited a bit and then went and tapped on the window! And when he called "Dick! Dick!" of course Dick thought it was he that he wanted, and he took the message and everything! And then the other man, the real Dick came along – and was too late to meet the first one. *Our* Dick had met him and got the message!'

Anne was quite breathless after this long speech. She sat and stared at the others eagerly. Didn't they think she was right?

They did, of course. Julian clapped her on the back. 'Well worked out, Anne! Of course that's what happened.'

Dick suddenly remembered the boy they had met on the way down from the old woman's cottage to Beacons Village – the whistling boy. What had he said about the old woman and her son?

'Anne – what did that whistling boy say? Wait a bit – he said that was Mrs Taggart's place – and he said we'd better not go there or her son would drive us off. And he said – yes, I remember now – he said "Dirty Dick we call him – he's a terror!" Dirty *Dick*! His name *must* be Dick then! Why didn't I think of it before?'

'That proves that Anne is right,' said Julian, pleased. Anne looked pleased too. It wasn't often that she thought of something clever before the others did!

They all sat thinking. 'Would this have anything to do with the escaped prisoner?' said George at last.

'It might,' said Julian. 'He might have been the prisoner himself, that fellow who came with the message. Did he say who the message was from?'

'Yes,' said Dick, trying to remember. 'He said it

was from Nailer. I think that was the name – but it was all given in whispers, you know.'

'A message from Nailer,' said Julian. 'Well – perhaps Nailer is in prison – a friend of the man who escaped. And maybe when he knew this fellow was going to make a dash for it, he gave him a message for someone – the man at that old cottage, son of the old woman. They may have had a prearranged plan.'

'How do you mean?' asked Dick, looking puzzled.

'Well – the old woman's son, Dirty Dick, may have known that when the bells rang out, this fellow was making a run for it – and would come to bring him a message. He was to wait in the barn at night if the bells rang, just in case it was Nailer's friend who had escaped.'

'Yes, I see,' said Dick. 'I think you're right. Yes, I'm sure you are. My word, I'm glad I didn't know that fellow at the window was an escaped convict!'

'And *you've* got the message from Nailer!' said Anne. 'What a peculiar thing! Just because we lost our way and went to the wrong place, you get a message from a prisoner given you by one who's escaped! It's a pity we don't know what the message means – or the paper either.'

'Had we better tell the police?' said George. 'I mean – it may be important. It might help them to catch that man.'

'Yes,' said Julian. 'I think we *should* tell the police. Let's have a look at our map. Where's the next village?'

He looked at the map for a minute. 'I think really we might as well go on with what I had planned,' he said. 'I planned we should reach this village here – Reebles, look – in time for lunch, in case we hadn't got sandwiches. We'd have gone there for drinks anyway. So I vote we just carry on with our ramble, and call in at

Reebles police station – if there is one – and tell them our bit of news.'

They all got up. Timmy was glad. He didn't approve of this long sit-down so soon after breakfast. He bounded ahead in delight.

'His leg's *quite* all right,' said Anne, pleased. 'Well I hope it teaches him not to go down rabbit holes again!'

It didn't, of course. He had his head down half a dozen within the next half-hour, but fortunately he could get no farther, and he was able to pull himself out quite easily.

The four saw little wild ponies that day. They came trotting over a hillock together, small and brown, with long manes and tails, looking very busy indeed. The children stopped in delight. The ponies saw them, tossed their pretty heads, turned one way all together and galloped off like the wind.

Timmy wanted to go after them, but George held his collar tightly. No one must chase those dear little wild ponies!

'Lovely!' said Anne. 'Lovely to meet them as suddenly as that. I hope we meet some more.'

The morning was as warm and sunny as the day before. Once again the four of them had to take off their blazers, and Timmy's tongue hung out, wet and dripping. The heather and wiry grass was soft underfoot. They followed the stream closely, liking its brown colour and its soft gurgling voice.

They bathed their hot feet in it as they ate one of their sandwiches at half past eleven. 'This is bliss!' said George, lying back on a tuft of heather with her feet lapped by the water. 'The stream is tickling my feet, and the sun is warming my face – lovely! Oh, get away, Timmy, you idiot! Breathing down my neck like that, and making my face so wet!'

The stream at last joined the path that led to the village of Reebles. They walked along it, beginning to think of dinner. It would be fun to have it in a little inn or perhaps a farmhouse, and keep their sandwiches for tea-time.

'But first we must find the police station,' said Julian. 'We'll get our tale told, and then we'll be ready for our meal!'

10 An angry policeman and
a fine lunch

There *was* a police station at Reebles, a small one with a house for the policeman attached. As the one policeman had four villages under his control he felt himself to be rather an important fellow.

He was in his house having his dinner when the children walked up to the police station. They found nobody there, and walked out again. The policeman had seen them from his window and he came out, wiping his mouth. He wasn't very pleased at having to come out in the middle of a nice meal of sausage and onions.

'What do you want?' he said, suspiciously. He didn't like children of any sort. Nasty little things, he thought them – always full of mischief and cheek. He didn't know which were worse, the small ones or the big ones!

Julian spoke to him politely. 'We've come to report something rather strange, which we thought perhaps the police ought to know. It might help them to catch the prisoner who escaped last night.'

'Ha!' said the policeman scornfully. 'You've seen him too, I suppose? You wouldn't believe how many people have seen him. 'Cording to them he's been in every part of the moor at one and the same time. Clever fellow he must be to split himself up like that.'

'Well, one of us saw him last night,' said Julian politely. 'At least, we think it must have been him. He gave a message to my brother here.'

'Ho, he did, did he?' said the policeman, eyeing Dick in a most disbelieving manner. 'So he runs about giving messages to school-boys, does he? And what message did he give you, may I ask?'

The message sounded extremely silly when Dick repeated it to the police. 'Two-Trees. Gloomy Water. Saucy Jane. And Maggie knows.'

'Really?' said the policeman, in a sarcastic voice. 'Maggie knows as well, does she? Well, you tell Maggie to come along here and tell me too. I'd like to meet Maggie – specially if she's a friend of yours.'

'She's not,' said Dick feeling annoyed. 'That was in the message. I don't know who Maggie is! How should I? We thought perhaps the police could unravel the meaning. We couldn't. The fellow gave me this bit of paper too.'

He handed the piece of dirty paper to the policeman, who looked at it with a crooked smile. 'So he gave you this too, did he?' he said. 'Now wasn't that kind of him? And what do you suppose all this is, scribbled on the paper?'

'We don't know,' said Dick. 'But we thought our report might help the police to catch the prisoner, that's all.'

'The prisoner's caught,' said the policeman, with a smirk on his face. 'You know so much – but you didn't know that! Yes, he's caught – four hours ago – and he's safe back in prison now. And let me tell you youngsters this – I'm not taken in by any silly school-boy spoofing, see?'

'It's not spoofing,' said Julian, in a very grown-up manner. 'You should learn to see the difference between the truth and a joke.'

That didn't please the policeman at all. He turned on Julian at once, his face reddening.

'Now you run away!' he said. 'I'm not having any cheek from you! Do you want me to take your names and addresses and report you?'

'If you like,' said Julian, in disgust. 'Have you got a notebook there? I'll give you all our names, and I myself will make a report to the police in our district when I get back.'

The policeman stared at him. He couldn't help being impressed by Julian's manner, and he calmed down a little.

'You go away, all of you,' he said, his voice not nearly so fierce. 'I shan't report you this time. But don't you go spreading silly stories like that or you'll get into trouble. Serious trouble too.'

'I don't think so,' said Julian. 'Anyway, seeing that you are not going to do anything about our story, may we have back our bit of paper, please?'

The policeman frowned. He made as if he would tear the paper up, but Dick snatched at it. He was too late. The aggravating policeman had torn it into four pieces and thrown it into the road!

'Don't you have laws against scattering litter in your village?' asked Dick, severely, and carefully picked up the four pieces of paper. The policeman glared at Dick as he put the bits into his pocket. Then he made a peculiar snorting noise, turned on his heel and marched back to his sausages and onions.

'And I hope his dinner's gone cold!' said George. 'Horrid fellow! Why should he think we're telling a lot of untruths?'

'It *is* rather an odd story of ours,' said Julian. 'After

all – *we* found it a bit difficult to believe when Dick first told it. I don't blame the policeman for disbelieving it – I blame him for his manner. It's a good thing most of our police aren't the same. Nobody would ever report anything.'

'He told us one bit of good news, anyway,' said Anne. 'That escaped prisoner is back in prison again! I'm so relieved to know that.'

'I am too,' said Dick. 'I didn't like the look of him at all. Well, Ju – what do we do now? Forget the whole business? Do *you* think there's anything in that message to follow up? And if so – can we do anything?'

'I don't know,' said Julian. 'We must think a bit. Let's go and see if we can scrounge a meal in some farmhouse somewhere. There seem to be plenty around.'

They asked a little girl if there was a farmhouse anywhere near that would give them dinner. She nodded and pointed.

'See that farmhouse up on the hill there? That's my gran's place. She'll give you dinner, I expect. She used to give dinner in the summer to trippers, and I expect she would give you some too, if you ask her, though it's late in the season.'

'Thanks,' said Julian, and they all went up the lane that curved round the hillside. Dogs barked loudly as they came near and Timmy's hackles went up at once. He growled.

'Friends, Timmy, friends,' said George. 'Dinner here, Timmy. Dinner, perhaps a nice bone for you. Bone!'

Timmy understood. The fur down his neck lay flat again and he stopped growling. He wagged his tail at the two dogs near the farm-gate who sniffed his doggy smell suspiciously even when he was some distance away.

A man hailed them. 'What do you kids want? Mind those dogs!'

'We wondered if we could get a meal here!' called back Julian. 'A little girl down in the village said we might.'

'I'll ask my mother,' said the man, and he yelled in an enormous voice to the farmhouse nearby. 'Ma! MA! Four kids out here want to know if you can give them a meal.'

A very fat old lady appeared, with twinkling eyes and red cheeks like an apple. She took one glance at the four by the gate, and nodded her head. 'Yes. They look decent children. Tell them to come along in. Better hold their dog's collar though.'

The four walked to the farmhouse, George holding Timmy firmly. The other two dogs came up, but as Timmy was hoping for a bone, he was determined to be friendly, and not a single growl came from him, even when the two dogs growled suspiciously. He wagged his tail, and let his tongue hang out.

The other dogs soon wagged theirs, and then it was safe to let Timmy go. He bounded over to them and there was a mad game of 'chase-me-roll-me-over' as George called it.

'Come your ways in,' said the plump old lady. 'Now you'll have to take what we've got. I'm busy today and haven't had time for cooking. You can have a bit of home-made meat-pie, or a slice or two of ham and tongue, or hard-boiled eggs and salad. Bless you, you look as pleased as Punch! I'll put the lot on the table for you and you can help yourselves! Will that do? There's no vegetables though. You'll have to make do with pickled cabbage and my own pickled onions and beetroot in vinegar.

'It sounds too marvellous for words,' said Julian. 'We shan't want any sweet after that!'

'There's no pudding today,' said the old lady. 'But I'll open a bottle or two of our own raspberries and you can have them with cream if you like. And there's the cream cheese I made yesterday too.'

'Don't tell us any more!' begged Dick. 'It makes me feel too hungry. Why is it that people on farms always have the most delicious food? I mean, surely people in towns can bottle raspberries and pickle onions and make cream cheese?'

'Well either they can't or they don't,' said George. 'My mother does all those things – and even when she lived in a town she did. Anyway, *I'm* going to when I'm grown-up. It must be so wonderful to offer home-made things by the score when people come to a meal!'

It was extraordinary to think that any children could possibly eat the meal the four did, after having had such a huge breakfast. Timmy ate an enormous dinner too, and then lay down with a sigh. How he wished he could live at that farmhouse! How lucky those other two dogs were!

A small girl came in shyly as they ate. 'I'm Meg,' she said. 'I live with my gran. What are your names?'

They told her. Then Julian had an idea. 'We're walking over your moor,' he said. 'We've been to lots of nice places. But there's one we haven't been to yet. Do you know it? It's called Two-Trees.'

The little girl shook her head. 'Gran would know,' she said. 'Gran! Where's Two-Trees?'

The old lady looked in at the door. 'What's that? Two-Trees? Oh, that was a lovely place once, but it's all in ruins now. It was built beside a strange dark lake, in the middle of the moors. Let's see now – what was it called?'

'Gloomy Water?' said Dick.

'Yes! That's right. Gloomy Water,' said the old lady. 'Are you thinking of going by there? You be careful then, there's marshland around there, just when you least expect it! Now – would you like anything more?'

'No thank you,' said Julian, regretfully, and paid the very modest bill. 'It's the nicest lunch we've ever had. Now we must be off.'

'Off to Two–Trees and Gloomy Water, I hope!' George whispered to Dick. 'That would be really exciting.'

11 Julian's idea

Once outside the farmhouse Julian looked round at the others. 'We'll find out how far Two-Trees is and see if we've got time to pay it a visit,' he said. 'If we have, we'll go along there and snoop round. If we haven't we'll go tomorrow.'

'How can we find out how far it is?' said Dick eagerly. 'Will it be on your map?'

'It may be marked there if the lake is big enough,' said Julian. They walked down the hill, and took a path that led once more over the moors. As soon as they were out of sight and hearing of anyone Julian stopped and took out his big map. He unfolded it and the four of them crouched over it as he spread it out on the heather.

'That nice old lady said it was in the middle of the moors,' said Julian. 'Also we know there's a lake or at any rate a big pool of some kind.'

His finger traced its way here and there on the map. Then George gave a cry and dabbed her finger down.

'There, look! It's not really in the middle. See – Gloomy Water! That must be it. Is Two-Trees marked as well?'

'No,' said Julian. 'But perhaps it wouldn't be if it's in ruins. Ruins aren't marked on maps unless they are important in some way. This can't be important. Well – that's certainly Gloomy Water marked there. What do you say? Shall we have a shot at going there this afternoon? I wonder exactly how far it is.'

'We could ask at the post-office,' said George. 'Probably once upon a time the postman had to take letters there. They might know. They could tell us the way to go.'

They went back to the village and found the post-office. It was part of the village store. The old man who kept it looked over the top of his glasses at the children.

'Gloomy Water! Now what be you wanting that for? A real miserable place it is, and it used to be so fine.

'What happened to it?' asked Dick.

'It was burnt,' said the old man. 'The owner was away, and only a couple of servants were there. It flared up one night, no one knows how or why – and was burnt almost to a shell. Couldn't get a fire-engine out there, you see. There was only a cart-track to the place.'

'And wasn't it ever built up again?' asked Julian. The old man shook his head.

'No. It wasn't worth it. The owner just let it fall to rack and ruin. The jackdaws and the owls nest there now, and the wild animals snuggle in the ruins. It's a queer place. I once went out to see it, hearing tales of lights being seen there. But there was nothing to see but the shell of the place, and the dark blue water. Ah, Gloomy Water's a good name for that lake!'

'Could you tell us the way? And how long would it take us to get there?' asked Julian.

'What for do you want to go and gaze at a poor old ruin?' said the old man. 'Or do you want to bathe in the lake? Well, don't you do so – it's freezing cold!'

'We just thought we'd go and see Gloomy Water,'

said Julian. 'Such a strange name. Which is the way, did you say?'

'I didn't say,' said the old fellow. 'But I will if you're so set on it. Where's your map? Is that one in your hand?'

Julian spread it out. The old fellow took a pen from his waistcoat pocket and began to trace a path over the moor. He put crosses here and there.

'See them crosses? They mark marshland. Don't go treading there, or you'll be up to your knees in muddy water! You follow these paths I've inked in for you and you'll be all right. Keep your eyes open for deer – there's plenty about those parts, and pretty things they are too.'

'Thank you very much,' said Julian, folding up the map. 'How long would it take us to get there from here?'

'Matter of two hours or more,' said the old man. 'Don't you try to go this afternoon. You'll find your-selves in darkness coming back, and with them dangerous marshy bits you're in danger all the time!'

'Right,' said Julian. 'Thanks very much. Er – we're thinking of doing a bit of camping, as the weather is so beautiful. I suppose you couldn't hire us a ground-sheet or two and a few rugs?'

The other three stared at him in astonishment. Camping out? Where? Why? What was Julian thinking of all of a sudden?

Julian winked at them. The old man was ferreting about in a cupboard. He pulled out two large rubber ground-sheets and four old rugs. 'Thought I had them somewhere!' he said. 'Well, better you camping out in October than me! Be careful you don't catch your deaths of cold!'

'Oh thanks – just what we want,' said Julian, pleased. 'Roll them up, you others. I'll settle up for them.'

Dick, Anne and George folded up the ground-sheets and the rugs in astonishment. Surely – surely Julian wasn't thinking of camping out by Gloomy Water? He must think the message that Dick had been given was very important!

'Julian!' said Dick, as soon as they got outside. 'What's up? What's all this for?'

Julian looked a little sheepish. 'Well – something suddenly came over me in the store,' he said. 'I suddenly felt we ought to go to Gloomy Water and snoop round. I felt excited somehow. And as we've got so little time this weekend I thought if we took things and camped out in the ruin we might make more of our few days.'

'What an idea!' said George. 'Not go on with our hiking, do you mean?'

'Well,' said Julian. 'If we find nothing, we *can* go on with our hike, of course. But if there's anything interesting, it's up to us to unearth it. I'm quite sure there's something up at Two-Trees.'

'We might meet Maggie there!' said Anne, with a giggle.

'We might!' said Julian. 'I feel quite free to go and investigate on our own seeing that we've made our report to the police, and it's been turned down with scorn. *Somebody* ought to follow up that message – besides Maggie!'

'Dear Maggie,' said Dick. 'I wonder who in the wide world she is!'

'Somebody worth watching if she's the friend of convicts,' said Julian, more soberly. 'Look, this is what I thought we'd do – buy some extra food, and go along to Gloomy Water this afternoon, arriving there before dark. We'll find a good place to shelter in – there must be some good spot in the old ruin – and get heather or bracken for beds. Then tomorrow we can be up bright and early to have a look round.'

'It sounds smashing,' said Dick, pleased. 'Sort of thing we like. What do you say, Tim?'

'Woof,' said Tim, solemnly, bumping his tail to and fro across Dick's legs.

'And if we find there's absolutely nothing of interest, well, we can come back here with the things we've borrowed, and go on with our hike,' said Julian. 'But we'll have to sleep the night there because it will be dark by the time we've had a look round.'

They bought some loaves of bread, some butter and potted meat, and a big fruit cake. Also some more chocolate and some biscuits. Julian bought a bottle of orangeade as well.

'There's sure to be a well,' he said. 'Or a spring of some sort. We can dilute the orangeade and drink it when we're thirsty. Now I think we're ready. Come on!'

They couldn't go as fast as usual because they were carrying so many things. Timmy was the only one that ran as fast as ever – but then Timmy carried nothing but himself!

It was a really lovely walk over the moorlands. They climbed fairly high and had wonderful views all over the autumn countryside. They saw wild ponies again, in the distance this time, and a little herd of dappled deer, that sped away immediately.

Julian was very careful to take the right paths – the ones traced so carefully on the map by the old man in the post-office. 'I expect he knew the way well because he was once a postman and had to take letters to Two-

Trees!' said Dick, bending over the map. 'We're getting on, Ju – halfway there!'

The sun began to sink low. The children hurried as much as they could because once the sun had gone darkness would soon come. Fortunately the sky was very clear, so twilight would be later than it had been the night before.

'It looks as if the moorland near here gives way soon to a little bit of wooded country, according to the map,' said Julian. 'We'll look out for clumps of trees.'

After another little stretch of moorland Julian pointed to the right 'Look!' he said. 'Trees! Quite a lot – a proper little wood.'

'And isn't that water over there?' said Anne. They stood still and gazed hard. Was it Gloomy Water? It might be. It looked such a dark blue. They hurried on eagerly. It didn't look very far now. Timmy ran ahead, his long tail waving in the air.

They went down a little winding path and joined a cart-track that was very much overgrown – so overgrown that it hardly looked like a track. 'This must lead to Two-Trees,' said Julian. 'I wish the sun wasn't going down so quickly. We'll hardly have any time to look round!'

They entered a wood. The track wound through it. The trees must have been cleared at some time to make a road through the wood. And then, quite suddenly, they came on what had once been the lovely house of Two-Trees.

It was a desolate ruin, blackened and scorched with fire. The windows had no glass, the roof had gone, except for a few rafters here and there. Two birds flew up with a loud cry as the children went near.

'Two Maggies!' said Anne, with a laugh. They were black and white magpies, their long tails stretched out behind them. 'I wonder if they know the message too.'

The house stood on the edge of the lake. Gloomy Water was indeed a good name for it. It lay there, smooth and dark, a curious deep blue. No little waves lapped the edge. It was as still as if it were frozen.

'I don't like it,' said Anne. 'I don't like this place at all! I wish we hadn't come!'

12   A hiding-place at Two-Trees

Nobody particularly liked the place. They all stared round and Julian pointed silently to something. At each end of the house was the great burnt trunk of a big tree.

'Those must be the two trees that gave the place its name,' said Julian. 'How horrid they look now, so stiff and black. Two-Trees and Gloomy Water – all so lonely and desolate now.'

The sun disappeared and a little chill came on the air. Julian suddenly became very busy. 'Come on – we must see if there's anywhere to shelter at all in this old ruin!'

They went to the silent house. The upper floors were all burnt out. The ground floor was pretty bad too, but Julian thought it might be possible to find a sheltered corner.

'This might do,' he said, coming out of a blackened room and beckoning the others to him. 'There is even a mouldy carpet still on the floor! And there's a big table. We could sleep under it if it rained – which I don't think it will do!'

'What a horrid room!' said Anne, looking round. 'I don't like its smell, either. I don't want to sleep here.'

'Well, find somewhere else then, but be quick about it,' said Julian. 'It will soon be dark. I'm going to collect heather and bracken straight away, before it's too dark. Coming, Dick and George?'

The three of them went off and came back with vast armfuls of heather and brown bracken. Anne met them, looking excited.

'I've found somewhere. Somewhere much better than this horrid room. Come and look.'

She took them to what once had been the kitchen. A door lay flat on the floor at the end of the room, and a stone stairway led downwards.

'That leads down to the cellars,' said Anne. 'I came in here and saw that door. It was locked and I couldn't open it. Well, I tugged and tugged and the whole door came off its rusty old hinges and tumbled down almost on top of me! And I saw there were cellars down there!'

She stared at Julian beseechingly. 'They'll be dry. They won't be burnt and black like everywhere else. We'll be well-sheltered. Can't we sleep down there? I don't like the feel of these horrid burnt rooms.'

'It's an idea,' said Julian. He switched on his torch and let the beam light up the cellar below. It seemed spacious and smelt all right.

He went down the steps, Timmy just in front. He called up in surprise.

'There's a proper room down here, as well as cellars all round. Maybe it was a kind of sitting-room for the staff. It's wired for electricity too – they must have had their own electricity generator. Yes – we'll certainly come down here.'

It was a strange little room. Moth-eaten carpets were on the floor, and the furnishings were moth-eaten too and covered with dust. Spiders had been at work and George slashed fiercely at the long cobwebs that hung down and startled her by touching her face.

'There are still candles in the candlesticks on this shelf!' said Dick, surprised. 'We can light them and have a bit of brightness when it's dark. This isn't bad at all. I must say I agree with Anne. There's something hateful about those burnt-out rooms.'

They piled heather and bracken into the cellar room on the floor. The furniture was so old and moth-eaten that it gave beneath their weight, and was useless for sitting on. The table was all right though. They soon set out their food on it after George had wiped it free of dust. She caused them all to have fits of choking because she was so vigorous in her dusting! They were driven up into the kitchen till the dust had settled.

It was dark outside now. The moon was not yet up. The wind rustled the dry leaves left on the trees around, but there was no lap-lap of water. The lake was as still as glass.

There was a cupboard in the cellar room. Julian opened it to see what was there. 'More candles – good!' he said, bringing out a bundle. 'And plates and cups. Did anyone see a well outside? If so we could dilute some orangeade and have a drink with our supper.'

No one had noticed a well – but Anne suddenly remembered something peculiar she had seen in a corner of the kitchen, near the sink.

'I believe I saw a pump up there!' she said. 'Go and see, Ju. If so, it might still work.'

He went up the cellar steps with a candle. Yes – Anne was right. That *was* an old pump over there in the corner. It probably pumped water into a tank and came out of the kitchen taps.

He turned on a big tap which was over the large sink. Then he took the handle of the pump and worked it vigorously up and down. Splash! Splash! Water came flooding through the big tap and splashed into the sink! That was good.

Julian pumped and pumped, feeling that he had better get rid of any water running into the tank for the first time for years. The tank might be dirty or rusty – he must wash it round with a good deal of pumped water first.

The water seemed to be clean and clear, and was certainly as cold as ice! Julian held a cup from the cellar cupboard under the tap, and then tasted the water. It was delicious.

'Good for you, Anne!' he called, going down the cellar steps with a cupful of water. 'Dick, you find some more cups – or a jug or something in that cupboard, and we'll wash them out and fill them with water for our orangeade.'

The cellar room looked very cheerful as Julian came down the steps. George and Anne had lit six more candles, and stuck them about here and there. The light they gave was very pleasant, and they also warmed the room a little.

'Well, I suppose as usual, everyone wants a meal?' said Julian. 'Good thing we bought that bread and potted meat and stuff. I can't say I'm as hungry as I was at breakfast, but I'm getting that way.'

The four squatted round on their beds of heather and bracken. They had put down their ground-sheets first in case the floor was damp, though it didn't seem to be. Over bread and butter and potted meat they discussed their plans. They would sleep there for the night and then have all the next day to examine Two-Trees and the lake.

'What exactly are we looking for?' asked Anne. 'Do you suppose there's some secret here, Julian?'

'Yes,' said Julian. 'And I think I know what it is!'

'What?' asked George and Anne, surprised. Dick thought he knew. Julian explained.

'Well, we know that a prisoner called Nailer sent an important message by his escaped friend to two people – one he wanted to send to Dirty Dick – but he didn't get it – and the other to Maggie, whoever she is. Now what secret does he want to tell them?'

'I think I can guess,' said Dick. 'But go on.'

'Now suppose that Nailer has done some big robberies,' said Julian. 'I don't know what. Jewellery robberies probably, because they are the commonest with big criminals. All right – he does a big robbery – he hides the stuff till he hopes the hue and cry will be over – but he's caught and put into prison for a number of years. But he doesn't tell where the stuff is hidden! He daren't even write a letter to tell his friends outside the prison where it is. All his letters are read before they leave the prison. So what is he to do?'

'Wait till someone escapes and then give him a message,' said Dick. 'And that's just what happened, isn't it, Julian? That round-headed man I saw was the escaped prisoner, and he was sent to tell Dirty Dick and Maggie where the stolen goods were hidden – so that they could get them before anyone else did!'

'Yes. I'm sure that's it,' said Julian. 'His friend, the escaped prisoner, probably wouldn't understand the message at all – but Dirty Dick and Maggie would, because they knew all about the robbery. And now Maggie will certainly try to find out where the stuff is.'

'Well, we must find it first!' said George, her eyes gleaming with excitement. 'We're here first, anyway. And tomorrow, as early as possible we'll begin to snoop round. What was the next clue in the message, Dick? After Two-Trees and Gloomy Water.'

'Saucy Jane,' said Dick.

'Sounds a silly sort of clue,' said Anne. 'Do you suppose Maggie and Jane are *both* in the secret?'

'Saucy Jane sounds more like a boat to me,' said Dick.

'Of *course*!' said George. 'A boat! Why not? There's a lake here, and I imagine that people don't build a house beside a lake unless they want to go boating and bathing and fishing. I bet we shall find a boat called Saucy Jane tomorrow – and the stolen goods will be inside it.'

'Too easy!' said Dick. 'And not a very clever place either. Anyone could come across goods hidden in a boat. No – Saucy Jane is a clue, but we shan't find the stolen goods in her. And remember, there's that bit of paper as well. It must have something to do with the hiding-place too, I should think.'

'Where is it?' asked Julian. 'That wretched policeman! He tore it up. Have you still got the pieces, Dick?'

'Of course,' said Dick. He fished in his pocket and brought them out. 'Four little pieces! Anyone got some gummed paper?'

Nobody had – but George produced a small roll of plaster. Strips were cut and stuck behind the four portions of paper. Now it was whole again. They all examined it carefully.

'Look – four lines drawn, meeting in the centre,' said Julian. 'At the outer end of each line there's a word, so faintly written I can hardly read one of them. What's this one? "Tock Hill." And this next one is "Steeple". Whatever are the others?'

They made them out at last. '"Chimney",' said Anne. 'That's the third.'

'And "Tall Stone" is the fourth,' said George. 'Whatever do they all mean? We shall never, never find out!'

'We'll sleep on it,' said Julian, cheerfully. 'It's

wonderful what good ideas come in the night. It will be a very interesting little problem to solve tomorrow!'

13   A night in the cellar

The piece of paper was carefully folded and this time Julian took it for safe keeping. 'I can't imagine what it means, but it's clearly important,' he said. 'We may quite suddenly come on something – or think of something – that will give us a clue to what the words and the lines mean on the paper.'

'We mustn't forget that dear Maggie has a copy of the paper too,' said Dick. 'She probably knows better than we do what it all means!'

'If she does, she will pay a visit to Two-Trees too,' said Anne. 'We ought to keep a look-out for her. Should we have to hide if we saw her?'

Julian considered this. 'No,' he said, 'I certainly don't think we should hide. Maggie can't *possibly* guess that we have had the message from Nailer, and the paper too. We had better just say we are on a hike and found this place and thought we would shelter here. All perfectly true.'

'And we can keep an eye on her, and see what she does if she comes!' said Dick, with a grin. 'Won't she be annoyed!'

'She wouldn't come alone,' said Julian, thoughtfully. 'I should think it quite likely that she would come with Dirty Dick! He didn't get the message, but she did – and probably part of her message was the statement that Dirty Dick would know everything too. So she would get in touch with him.'

'Yes – and be surprised that he hadn't got the message or the paper,' said George. 'Still, they'd think that the escaped fellow hadn't been able to get to Dirty Dick.'

'All very complicated,' said Anne, yawning. 'I can't follow any more arguments and explanations – I'm half asleep. How long are you going to be before you settle down?'

Dick yawned too. 'I'm coming now,' he said. 'My bed of bracken and heather looks inviting. It's not at all cold in here, is it?'

'The only thing I don't like is the thought of those cellars beyond this little underground room,' said Anne. 'I keep thinking that Maggie and her friends might be there, waiting to pounce on us when we are asleep.'

'You're silly,' said George, scornfully. '*Really* silly! Do you honestly suppose that Timmy would lie here quietly if there was anyone in those cellars? You know jolly well he would be barking his head off!'

'Yes. I know all that,' said Anne, snuggling down in her heathery bed. 'It's just my imagination. You haven't got any, George, so you don't bother about imaginary fears. I'm not *really* scared while Timmy is here. But I do think it's funny the way we always plunge into something peculiar when we're together.'

'Adventures always do come to some people,' said Dick. 'You've only got to read the lives of explorers and see how they simply *walk* into adventures all the time.'

'Yes, but I'm not an explorer,' said Anne. 'I'm an ordinary person, and I'd be just as pleased if things *didn't* keep happening to me.'

The others laughed. 'I don't expect anything much will happen this time,' said Julian, comfortingly. 'We go back to school on Tuesday and that's not far off. Not much time for anything to happen!'

He was wrong of course. Things can happen one after the other in a few minutes! Still, Anne cuddled down feeling happier. This was better than last night when she was all alone in that horrid little loft. Now she had all the others with her, Timmy too.

Anne and George had one big bed between them. They drew their two rugs over themselves, and put their blazers on top too. Nobody had undressed because Julian had said that they might be too cold in just their night things.

Timmy as usual put himself on George's feet. She moved them because he was heavy. He wormed his way up the bed and found a very comfortable place between the knees of the two girls. He gave a heavy sigh.

'That means he's planning to go to sleep!' said George. 'Are you quite comfortable, Anne?'

'Yes,' said Anne, sleepily. 'I like Timmy there. I feel safe!'

Julian was blowing out the candles. He left just one burning. Then he got into his bed of bracken and heather beside Dick. He felt tired too.

The four slept like logs. Nobody moved except Timmy, who got up once or twice in the night and sniffed round inquiringly. He had heard a noise in the cellars. He stood at the closed door that led to the cellars and listened, his head on one side.

He sniffed at the crack. Then he went back to bed, satisfied. It was only a toad! Timmy knew the smell of toads. If toads liked to crawl about in the night, they were welcome to!

The second time he awoke he thought he heard something up in the kitchen above. He padded up the steps, his paws making a click-click-click as he went. He stood in the kitchen silently, his eyes gleaming like green lamps, as the moon shone on him.

An animal with a long bushy tail began to slink away outside the house. It was a fine fox. It had smelt unusual smells near the old ruin – the scent of people and of a dog, and it had come to find out what was happening.

It had slunk into the kitchen and then smelt the strong scent of Timmy in the room below. As quietly as a cat it had slunk out again – but Timmy had awakened!

Now the dog stood watching and waiting – but the fox had gone! Timmy sniffed its scent and padded to the door. He debated whether to bark and go after the fox.

The scent grew very faint, and Timmy decided not to make a fuss. He padded back to the steps that led down to the cellar room, and curled up on George's feet again. He was very heavy, but George was too tired to wake up and push him off. Timmy lay with one ear cocked for a while, and then went to sleep again, with his ear still cocked. He was a good sentinel!

It was dark in the cellar when the one candle went out. There was no daylight or sunshine to wake the children down in that dim little room, and they slept late.

Julian woke up first. He found his bed suddenly very hard, and he turned over to find a comfortable place. The heather and bracken had been flattened with his weight, and the floor below was very hard indeed! The movement woke him up, and he lay blinking in the darkness. Where was he?

He remembered at once and sat up. Dick woke too and yawned. 'Dick! It's half past eight!!' said Julian, looking at the luminous hands of his wrist-watch. 'We've slept for hours and hours!'

They rolled out of their heathery bed. Timmy leapt off George's feet and came over to them, his tail wagging gladly. He had been half-awake for a long time and was very glad to see Julian and Dick awake too, because he was thirsty.

The girls awoke – and soon there was a great deal of noise and activity going on. Anne and George washed at the big stone sink, the cold water making them squeal. Timmy lapped up a big bowlful of water gladly. The boys debated whether or not to have a splash in the lake. They felt very dirty.

Dick shivered at the thought. 'Still, I think we ought to,' he said. 'Come on, Ju!'

The two boys went down to the lake-side and leapt in. It was icy-cold! They swam out out strongly and came back glowing and shouting.

By the time they were back the girls had got breakfast in the cellar room. It was darker than the kitchen, but all of them disliked the look of the burnt, scorched rooms above. The bread and butter, potted meat, cake and chocolate went down well.

In the middle of the meal a sound came echoing into the old house – bells! Anne stopped eating, and her heart beat fast.

But they were not the clanging warning bells she had heard before!

'Church bells,' said Julian at once, seeing Anne's sudden look of fright. 'Lovely sound I always think!'

'Oh *yes*,' said Anne, thankfully. 'So it is. It's Sunday and people are going to church. I'd like to go too, on this lovely sunny October day.'

'We might walk across the moor to the nearest

village if you like,' said Dick, looking at his watch. 'But we should be very late.'

It was decided that it was much too late. They pushed their plates aside and planned what to do that day.

'The first thing, of course, is to see if there's a boat-house and find out if there's a boat called *Saucy Jane*,' said Julian. 'Then we'd better try and puzzle out what that plan means. We could wander here and there and see if we can find Tall Stone – and I'll look at the map to see if Tock Hill is marked. That was on the plan too, wasn't it?'

'You boys go and get some more heather and bracken while we clear away and wash up,' said Anne. 'That is if you mean us to camp here another night.'

'Yes. I think we will,' said Julian. 'I think we may find things rather interesting here this weekend!'

Julian went out with Dick and they brought in a great deal more bedding. Everyone had complained that the hard floor came through the amount of heather and bracken they had used the night before, and poor George was quite stiff.

The girls took the dirty things up to the big sink to wash them. There was nothing to dry them with but that didn't matter. They laid them on the old worn draining board to dry.

They wiped their hands on their hankies and then felt ready for exploring round outside. The boys were ready too.

With Timmy bounding here and there they went down to the lake. A path had once led down to it, with a low wall on each side. But now the wall was broken, moss had crept everywhere, and the path was choked with tufts of heather and even with small bushes of gorse.

The lake was as still and dark as ever. Some moor-hens chugged across it quickly, disappearing under the water when they saw the children.

'Now, what about the boat-house?' said Dick at last. 'Is there one – or not?'

14   *Where is the* Saucy Jane?

They walked beside the lake as best they could. It was difficult because bushes and trees grew right down to the edge. It seemed as if there was no boat-house at all.

And then George came to a little backwater, leading off the lake. 'Look!' she called. 'Here's a sort of river running from the lake.'

'It's not a river. It's only a little backwater,' said Dick. 'Now we *may* find a boat-house somewhere here.'

They followed the backwater a little way, and then Julian gave an exclamation. 'There it is! But it's so covered up with ivy and brambles that you can hardly see it!'

They all looked where he pointed. They saw a long low building built right across the backwater, where it narrowed and came to an end. It was almost impossible to tell that it was a building, it was so overgrown.

'That's it!' said Dick, pleased. 'Now for the *Saucy Jane!*'

They scrambled through bushes and brambles to get to the entrance of the building. It had to be entered by the front, which was over the water and completely open. A broad ledge ran right round the boat-house inside, and the steps that went up to it from the bank outside were all broken away, completely rotted.

'Have to tread warily here,' said Julian. 'Let me go first.'

He tried the old wooden steps, but they gave way beneath him at once. 'Hopeless!' he said. 'Let's see if there's any other way into the boat-house.'

There wasn't – but at one side some of the wooden boards that made the wall of the boat-house were so rotten that they could be pulled away to make an opening. The boys pulled them down and then Julian squeezed through the opening into the dark, musty boat-house.

He found himself on the broad ledge that went round the great shed. Below him was the dark, quiet water with not even a ripple on it. He called to the others.

'Come along in! There's a wooden ledge to stand on here, and it's hardly rotted at all. It must be made of better wood.'

They all went through the opening and stood on the ledge, peering down. Their eyes had to get used to the darkness at first, because the only light came through the big entrance at the farther end – and that was obscured by big trails of ivy and other creepers hanging down from roof to water.

'There *are* boats here!' said Dick, excited. 'Tied up to posts. Look – there's one just below us. Let's hope one of them is the *Saucy Jane!*'

There were three boats. Two of them were half full of water, and their bows were sunk right down. 'Must have got holes in them,' said Julian, peering about. He had got out his torch and was shining it all round the old boat-house.

Oars were strung along the walls. Dirty, pulpy masses of something lay on the shelves too – rotted cushions probably. A boat-hook stood in one corner. Ropes were in coils on a shelf. It was a dreary desolate sight, and Anne didn't like the strange echoes of their voices in the damp-smelling, lonely boat-house.

'Let's see if any of the boats are called *Saucy Jane*,' said Dick. He flashed his torch on to the nearest one. The name was almost gone.

'What is it?' said Dick, trying to decipher the faded letters. '*Merry* something.'

'*Meg*!' said Anne. '*Merry Meg*. Well, she may be a sister of *Saucy Jane*. What's the next boat's name?'

The torch shone steadily on to it. The name there was easier to read. They all read it at once.

'*Cheeky Charlie*!'

'Brother to *Merry Meg*!' said Dick. 'Well, all I can say is that these poor old boats look anything but merry or cheeky.'

'I'm sure the last one must be *Saucy Jane*!' said Anne, excited. 'I do hope it is!'

They went along the broad ledge and tried to read the name on the half-sunk boat there. 'It begins with C,' said George, disappointed. 'I'm sure it's C.'

Julian took out his handkerchief and dipped it in the water. He rubbed at the name to try and clean it and make it clearer.

It could be read then – but it wasn't *Saucy Jane*!

'*Careful Carrie*!' read the four, mournfully. 'Blow!'

'*Merry Meg*, *Cheeky Charlie*, *Careful Carrie*,' said Julian. 'Well, it's quite obvious that *Saucy Jane* belongs to the family of boats here – but where oh where is she?'

'Sunk out of sight?' suggested Dick.

'Don't think so,' said Julian. 'The water is pretty shallow in this boat-house – it's right at the very end of the little backwater, you see. I think we should be able to spot a boat sunk to the bottom. We can see the sandy bottom of the backwater quite clearly by the light of our torches.'

Just to make quite sure they walked carefully all round the broad wooden ledge and flashed their torches on the water that filled the boat-house. There was no completely sunken boat there at all.

'Well, that's that,' said Dick. 'The *Saucy Jane* is gone. Where? Why? And when?'

They flashed their torches round the walls of the boat-house once more. George's eye was caught by a large flat wooden thing standing upright on the ledge at one side of the house.

'What's that?' she said. 'Oh – a raft, isn't it? That's what those paddles are for, then, that I saw on the shelf above.'

They went and examined the raft. 'Yes – and in quite good condition too,' said Julian. 'It would be rather fun to see if it would carry us on the water.'

'Ooooh *yes*!' said Anne, thrilled. 'That would be super. I always like rafts. I'd rather try that raft than any of those boats.'

'Well, there's only one boat that is possible to use,' said Julian. 'The others are obviously no good – they must have big holes in them to sink down like that.'

'Hadn't we better look into them carefully just to make sure there's no loot hidden there?' said Dick.

'If you like,' said Julian. 'But *I* think it's *Saucy Jane* that's got the loot – otherwise why mention it by name in that message?'

Dick felt that Julian was right. All the same he went to examine the three boats most methodically. But except for rotted and burst cushions and coils of rope there was nothing to be seen in the boats at all.

'Well – where's the *Saucy Jane*?' said Dick, puzzled. 'All the family are here but her. Can she be hidden anywhere on the banks of the lake?'

'*That's* an idea!' said Julian, who was trying to shift

the big raft. 'That's a really good idea! I think we ought
to explore all round the lake and see if we can find the
Saucy Jane hidden anywhere.'

'Let's leave the raft for a bit then,' said George,
feeling thrilled at the thought of possibly finding the
Saucy Jane tucked away somewhere, all the loot hidden
in her. 'Let's go now!'

They made their way round the wooden ledge to the
opening they had made in the side of the boat-house,
and jumped down. Timmy leapt down gladly. He
hadn't liked the dark boat-house at all. He ran into the
warm sunshine, wagging his tail.

'Now which side of the lake shall we go to first?'
said Anne. 'The left or the right?'

They went down to the edge of the silent water and
looked to left and right. They both seemed to be
equally thick with bushes!

'It's going to be difficult to keep close to the edge of
the water,' said Julian. 'Anyway, we'll try. The left
side looks a bit easier. Come on!'

It was fairly easy at first to keep close to the water,
and examine any tiny creek or look under overhanging bushes. But after about a quarter of a mile the
undergrowth became so very thick and grew so close
to the water's edge that it was quite impossible to force
their way through it without completely ruining their
clothes.

'I give up!' said Julian at last. 'I shall have no jersey
left in a minute! These spiteful brambles! My hands are
ripped to bits.'

'Yes – they *are* spiteful!' said Anne. 'I felt that too!'

Timmy was the only one really enjoying himself.
He couldn't *imagine* why the four were scrambling
through such thick undergrowth, but as it was just
what he liked he was very pleased. He was disap-

pointed when they decided to give up and go back.

'Shall we try the right hand side of the lake, do you think?' said Julian, as they went back, rather disheartened.

'No. Don't let's,' said Anne. 'It looks even worse than this side. It's only a waste of time. I'd rather go out on the raft!'

'Well – that would surely be a better way of exploring the banks of the lake than scrambling through prickly bushes, wouldn't it?' said George. 'We'd only need to paddle along slowly and squint into all the little creeks and under overhanging trees – it would be easy!'

'Of course,' said Dick. 'We were silly not to think of it before. It would be a lovely way of spending the afternoon, anyway.'

They came through the trees and saw the ruined house in the distance. Timmy suddenly stopped. He gave a low growl, and all the others stopped too.

'What's up, Timmy?' said George in a low voice. 'What is it?'

Timmy growled again. The others cautiously retreated behind bushes aand looked intently towards the house. They could see nothing out of the way. Nobody seemed to be about. Then what was Timmy growling at?

And then a woman came in sight, and with her was a man. They were talking earnestly together.

'Maggie! I bet it's Maggie!' said Julian.

'And the other is Dirty Dick,' said Dick. 'I recognise him – yes – it's Dirty Dick.'

15 Maggie – and Dirty Dick

They watched the couple in the distance, and thought quickly. Julian had been expecting them, so he was not surprised. Dick was looking at Dirty Dick, recognising the broad, short man, with his hunched-up shoulders and shock of hair. He didn't like the look of him any more than when he had seen him up at the old cottage!

Anne and George didn't like the look of the woman either! She was wearing trousers and had a jacket draped round her shoulders. She was also wearing sun-glasses, and smoking a cigarette. She walked quickly and they could hear her voice. It was sharp and determined.

'So that's Maggie,' thought Julian. 'Well, I don't like her. She looks as hard as nails – a good companion for Nailer!'

He moved cautiously towards the other three. George had her hand on Timmy's collar, afraid that he might show himself.

'Listen,' said Julian. 'You're none of you to turn a hair! We'll just walk out into the open, talking cheerfully together and let them see us. If they ask us what we're doing, you all know what to say. Chatter nonsense as much as you like – put them off and make them think we're a bunch of harmless kids. If there are any leading questions asked us – leave *me* to answer them. Ready?'

They nodded. Then Julian swung out from the bushes and walked into the open, calling to Dick. 'Here we are again – there's the old house! My word, it looks worse than ever this morning!'

George and Timmy came bounding out together, and Anne followed, her heart beating fast. She wasn't as good as the others at this sort of thing!

The man and the woman stopped abruptly when they saw the children. They said a few words to one another very rapidly. The man scowled.

The children went towards them, chattering all the time as Julian had ordered. The woman called sharply to them.

'Who are you? What are you doing here?'

'Just hiking,' said Julian, stopping. 'It's our half-term.'

'What do you want to come *here* for then?' asked the woman. 'This is private property.'

'Oh no,' said Julian. 'It's only a burnt-out ruin. Anyone can come. We want to explore this strange lake – it looks exciting.'

The man and the woman looked at one another. It was clear that the idea of the children exploring the lake was surprising and annoying to them. The woman spoke again.

'You can't explore this lake. It's dangerous. People are forbidden to bathe in it or use a boat.'

'We weren't told that,' said Julian, looking astonished. 'We were told how to get here, and no one said the lake was forbidden. You've been told wrongly.'

'We want to watch the moorhens, you see,' put in Anne, suddenly seeing a moorhen on the water. 'We're fond of nature.'

'And we've been told there are deer near here,' said George.

'And wild ponies,' said Dick. 'We saw some yesterday. They were really lovely. Have you seen any?'

This sudden burst of chatter seemed to annoy the man and the woman more than Julian's answers. The man spoke roughly.

'Stop this nonsense. People aren't allowed here. Clear out before we make you!'

'Why are *you* here, then, if people aren't allowed?' asked Julian, and a hard tone came into his voice. 'Don't talk to us like that.'

'You clear off, I say!' cried the man, suddenly shouting loudly as he lost his temper. He took two or three steps towards them, looking very threatening indeed. George loosed her hold on Timmy's collar.

Timmy also took two or three steps forward. His hackles went up and he emitted a most fearsome growl. The man stopped suddenly, and then retreated.

'Take hold of that dog's collar,' he ordered. 'He looks savage.'

'Then he looks what he is,' said George. 'I'm not taking hold of his collar while you're about. Don't think it!'

Timmy took two or three more steps forward, growling loudly, walking stiffly and menacingly. The woman called out at once.

'It's all right, children. My friend here just lost his temper for a moment. Call your dog back.'

'Not while you are about,' said George. 'How long are you staying?'

'What's that to do with you?' growled the man, but he didn't say any more because Timmy at once growled back.

'Let's go and have something to eat,' said Julian,

loudly, to the others. 'After all, we have as much right to be here as these people have. We don't need to take any notice of them – and we shan't be in *their* way!'

The four children marched forward. Timmy was still loose. He barked savagely once or twice as he came close to the unpleasant couple, and they shrank back at once. Timmy was such a big dog and he looked so very powerful! They eyed the children angrily as they went by, and watched them go into the ruined house.

'On guard, Timmy,' said George, as soon as they were in, pointing to the ruined doorway. Timmy understood at once, and stood in the doorway, a menacing figure with hackles up and snarling mouth. The children went down to the cellar room. They looked round to see if anyone had been there while they were away, but nothing seemed to have been moved.

'They probably haven't even noticed the cellars,' said Julian. 'I hope there's plenty of bread left. I'm hungry. I wish to goodness we were going to have a dinner like the one we had yesterday! I say – what an unpleasant pair Maggie and Dick are!'

'Yes. Very,' said Dick. 'I can't bear Maggie. Horrid mean voice and hard face. Ugh!'

'I think Dirty Dick is worse,' said Anne. 'He looks like a gorilla or something with his broad hunched-up body. And WHY doesn't he cut his hair?'

'Fancies himself like that, I expect,' said George, cutting a loaf of bread. 'His surname ought to be Hairy. Or Tarzan. I'm jolly glad we've got Timmy.'

'So am I,' said Anne. 'Good old Timmy. He hated them, didn't he? I bet they won't come near the doorway with Timmy there!'

'I wonder where they are,' said Dick picking up a

great hunk of bread and butter and potted meat. 'I'm going to look.'

He came back in half a minute. 'They've gone to the boat-house, I think,' he said. 'I just caught a sight of one of them moving in that direction. Looking for *Saucy Jane*, I expect.'

'Let's sit down and eat and talk over what we'll do next,' said Julian. 'And what we think *they* will do next! That's quite important. They may be able to read the clues on that paper better than we can. If we watch what they do it may give us a guide as to what *we* must do.'

'That's true,' said Dick. 'I imagine that the plan Nailer sent must mean something to Dirty Dick and Maggie, just as the message did.' He chewed at his bread, thinking hard, trying once more to fathom the meaning of that mysterious piece of paper.

'I think on the whole we will follow out our original plan for this afternoon,' said Julian, after a little silence. 'We'll get out that raft and go on the lake with it. It's a harmless looking thing to do. We can examine the banks as we go – and if Maggie and Dick are out in a boat too, we can keep an eye on them as well.'

'Yes. Good idea,' said George. 'It's a heavenly afternoon anyway. I'd love to paddle about on the lake with that raft. I hope it's good and sound.'

'Sure to be,' said Dick. 'The wood it's made of is meant to last. Pass the cake, George – and *don't* save Timmy any. It's wasted on him.'

'It isn't!' said George. 'You know he loves it.'

'Yes. But I still say it's wasted on him,' said Dick. 'Good thing we got such an enormous cake! Are there any biscuits left?'

'Plenty,' said Anne. 'And chocolate too!'

'Good,' said Dick. 'I only hope our food will last

us out. It won't if George has her usual colossal appetite.'

'What about yours?' said George, indignantly, rising every time to Dick's lazy teasing.

'Shut up, you two,' said Julian. 'I'm going to fill the water jug and have some orangeade. Give me something to take to old Tim.'

They spent about half an hour over their lunch. Then they decided to go and tackle the raft in the boat-house, and see if they could possibly launch it on the lake. It would be heavy, they knew.

They left the old house and went off to the boat-house. Julian suddenly caught sight of something out on the lake.

'Look!' he said, 'they've got one of the boats out of the boat-house – the one that wasn't half-sunk, I suppose! Dirty Dick is rowing hard. I BET they're looking for the *Saucy Jane*!'

They all stood still and watched. Dick's heart sank. Would Maggie and Dirty Dick get there first, and find what he and the other three were looking for? Did they know where the *Saucy Jane* was?

'Come on,' said Julian. 'We'd better get going if we want to keep an eye on them. They may be rowing to where the *Saucy Jane* is hidden!'

They climbed in through the wooden side of the boat-house and went to the raft. Julian saw at once that one of the boats had gone – *Merry Meg*. It was the only boat that was fit to take.

The four began to manhandle the big raft. They took it to the edge of the ledge. It had rope-handles on each side which the children held on to.

'Now – ease her gently,' said Julian. 'Gently does it. Down she goes!'

And down she went, landing with a big splash in the

water. She bobbed there gently, a strong, sound raft, eager to go out on the lake!

'Get the paddles,' said Julian. 'Then we'll be off.'

16 Out on the raft

There were four little paddles. Dick got them, and gave everyone one each. Timmy looked down solemnly at the raft. What was it? Surely he was not expected to ride on that bobbing, floating thing?

Julian was on the raft already, holding it steady for the others. He helped Anne on and then George stepped down. Dick came last – well, not quite last, because Timmy was not yet on.

'Come on, Tim!' said George. 'It's all right! It's not the kind of boat you're used to, but it acts in the same way. Come *on*, Timmy!'

Timmy jumped down and the raft bobbed violently. Anne sat down suddenly with a giggle. 'Oh dear – Timmy is so *sudden*! Keep still, Tim – there isn't enough room on this raft for you to walk all over it.'

Julian pushed the raft out of the boat-house. It knocked against the wooden ledge as it went, and then swung out on to the backwater outside. It floated very smoothly.

'Here we go!' said Julian, paddling deftly. 'I'll steer, Dick. None of you need to paddle till I say so. I can paddle and steer at the moment, till we get on to the lake itself.'

They were all sitting on the raft except Timmy, who was standing up. He was very interested in seeing the water flow past so quickly. *Was* this a boat then?

He was used to boats – but in boats the water was never quite so near. Timmy put out a paw into the water. It was pleasantly cool and tickled him. He lay down with his nose almost in the water.

'You're a funny dog, Timmy!' said Anne. 'You won't get up too suddenly, will you, or you'll knock me overboard.'

Julian paddled down the little backwater and the raft swung out on to the lake itself. The children looked to see if there was any sign of Maggie and Dirty Dick.

'There they are!' said Julian. 'Out in the middle, rowing hard. Shall we follow them? If they know where the *Saucy Jane* is they'll lead us to it.'

'Yes. Follow them,' said Dick. 'Shall *we* paddle now? We'll have to be quick or we may lose them.'

They all paddled hard, and the raft suddenly swung to and fro in a most alarming manner.

'Hey, stop!' shouted Julian. 'You're all paddling against one another. We're going round in circles. Dick and Anne go one side and George the other. That's better. Watch how we're going, all of you, and stop paddling for a moment if the raft swings round too much.'

They soon got into the way of paddling so that the raft went straight ahead. It was fun. They got very hot and wished they could take off their jerseys. The sun was quite warm, and there was no wind at all – it was really a perfect October afternoon.

'They've stopped rowing,' said George, suddenly. 'They're looking at something – do you suppose they have got a bit of paper like the one we have, with the same marks, and are examining it? I *wish* I could see!'

They all stopped paddling and looked towards the boat in which Maggie and Dirty Dick sat. They were certainly examining something very carefully – their heads were close together. But they were too far away for the children to see if they were holding a piece of paper.

'Come on – we'll get as close to them as we can!' said Julian, beginning to paddle again. 'I expect it will make them absolutely mad to see us so close, but we can't help that!'

They paddled hard again, and at last came up to the boat. Timmy barked. Maggie and Dirty Dick at once looked round and saw the raft and the four children. They stared at them savagely.

'Hallo!' cried Dick, waving a paddle. 'We took the raft out. It goes well. Does your boat go all right?'

Maggie went red with rage. 'You'll get into trouble for taking that raft without permission,' she shouted.

'Whose permission did *you* ask when you took that boat?' shouted back Julian. 'Tell us and we'll ask their permission to use this raft!'

George laughed. Maggie scowled, and Dirty Dick looked as if he would like to throw his oars at them.

'Keep away from us!' he shouted. 'We don't want you kids spoiling our afternoon!'

'We like to be friendly!' called Dick, and made George laugh again.

Maggie and Dirty Dick had a hurried and angry conversation. They glared at the raft and then Maggie gave an order to Dirty Dick. He took up the oars again, and began to row, looking rather mutinous.

'Come on – follow,' said Julian, so the four began to paddle again following after the boat. 'Maybe we'll learn something now.'

But they didn't. Dirty Dick rowed the boat towards the west bank, and the raft followed. Then he swung out into the middle again, and again the raft followed, the children panting in their efforts to keep up.

Dirty Dick rowed right across to the east bank and stayed there till the children came up. Then he rowed off again.

'Having some nice exercise, aren't you?' called the woman in her harsh voice. 'So good for you all!'

The boat swung out to the middle of the lake again. Dick groaned. 'Blow! My arms are so tired I can hardly paddle. What are they doing?'

'I'm afraid they're just leading us on a wild goose chase,' said Julian, ruefully. 'They have evidently made up their minds that they won't look for the *Saucy Jane* while we're about – they're just tiring us out!'

'Well, if *that's* what they're doing I'm not playing!' said Dick, and he put down his paddle and lay flat on his back, his knees drawn up, panting hard.

The others did the same. They were all tired. Timmy licked each one sympathetically and then sat down on George. She pushed him off so violently that he nearly fell into the water.

'Timmy! Right on my middle!' cried George, surprised and indignant. 'You great clumsy dog, you!'

Timmy licked her all over, shocked at being scolded by George. She was too exhausted to push him away.

'What's happened to the boat?' asked Anne at last. 'I'm too tired to sit up and see.'

Julian sat up, groaning. 'Oh my back! Now where is that wretched boat? Oh, there it is – right away down the lake, making for the landing-place by the house – or for the boat-house probably. They've given up the search for the *Saucy Jane* for the time being anyway.'

'Thank goodness,' said Anne. 'Perhaps we can give it up too – till tomorrow anyhow! Stop snuffling down my neck, Timmy. What do you want us to do, Julian?'

'I think we'd better get back,' said Julian. 'It's too late now to start searching the banks of the lake – and anyway somehow I think it wouldn't be much use. The two in the boat didn't appear to be going anywhere near the banks – except when they began to play that trick on us to make us tired out!'

'Well, let's get back then,' said George. 'But I simply must have a rest first. Timmy, I shall push you into the water if you keep sitting on my legs.'

There was a sudden splash. George sat up in alarm. Timmy was not on the raft!

He was swimming in the water, looking very pleased with himself.

'There! He thought he'd rather jump in than be pushed,' said Dick, grinning at George.

'*You* pushed him in!' said George, looking fierce.

'I didn't,' said Dick. 'He just took a header. He's having a jolly good time. I say – what about putting a rope round him and getting him to pull us to shore? It would save an awful lot of paddling.'

George was just about to say what she thought of *that* idea, when she caught Dick's sly grin. She kicked out at him.

'Don't keep baiting me, Dick. I'll push *you* in, in a minute.'

'Like to try?' asked Dick, at once. 'Come on. I'd like a wrestle to see who'd go into the water first.'

George, of course, always rose to a challenge. She never could resist one. She was up in a moment and fell on Dick, who very nearly went overboard at once.

'Shut up, you two!' said Julian, crossly. 'We haven't got a change of clothing, you know that. And I don't want to take you back with bronchitis or pneumonia. Stop it, George.'

George recognised the tone in his voice and she stopped. She ran her hand through her short curls and gave a sudden grin.

'All right, Teacher!' she said, and sat down meekly. She picked up her paddle.

Julian picked up his. 'We'll get back,' he said. 'The sun's sinking low. It seems to slide down the sky at a most remarkable speed in October.'

They took a very wet Timmy on board and began to paddle back. Anne thought it was a truly lovely evening. She gazed dreamily round as she paddled. The lake was a wonderful dark blue, and the ripples they made turned to silver as they ran away from the raft. Two moorhens said 'crek-crek' and swam round the raft in curiosity, their heads bobbing like clockwork.

Anne gazed over the tops of the trees that grew at the lake-side. The sky was turning pink. Away in the distance, on a high slope about a mile away she saw something that interested her.

It looked like a high stone. She pointed at it. 'Look, Julian,' she said. 'What's that stone? Is it a boundary mark, or something? It must be very big.'

Julian looked where she was pointing. 'Where?' he said. 'Oh, that. I can't imagine what it is.'

'It looks like a very tall stone,' said Dick, suddenly catching sight of it too.

'A tall stone,' repeated Anne, wondering where she had heard that before. 'A tall . . . oh, of *course*! It was printed on that plan, wasn't it – on the piece of paper Dick was given. Tall Stone! Don't you remember?'

'Yes. So it was,' said Dick and he stared at the far-away stone monument with interest. Then as the raft swung onwards, high trees hid the stone. It was gone.

'Tall Stone,' said Julian. 'It may be only a coincidence, of course. It wants a bit of thinking about, though. Funny we should suddenly spot it.'

'Would the loot be buried there?' asked George,

doubtfully. Julian shook his head. 'Oh, no,' he said, 'it is probably hidden in some position explained by that mysterious map. Paddle up, everyone! We really must get back.'

17 Tit for tat!

When they arrived at the boat-house there was no sign of Maggie or Dick. But their boat was in the shed, tied up in front of the other two, where it had been before.

'They're back all right,' said Julian. 'I wonder where they are. Don't let's drag this clumsy, heavy raft into the boat-house. I don't feel as if I've any strength left in my arms. Let's drag it under a bush and tie it there.'

They thought this a good idea. They pulled the raft up to some thick bushes and tied it firmly to a root that was sticking out of the ground.

Then they made their way to the ruined house, keeping a sharp look-out for Maggie and Dick. There was still no sign of them.

They went in, Timmy first. He didn't growl so they knew it was safe. He led the way to the cellar steps. Then he growled!

'What's up?' said Julian. 'Are they down there, Tim?'

Timmy ran straight down the steps into the cellar room. He growled again, but it was not the fierce growl he always gave when he wanted to warn that enemies or strangers were near. It was an angry, annoyed growl as if something was wrong.

'I expect dear Maggie and Dirty Dick have been down here and found out where our headquarters are!' said Julian, following Timmy down the steps. He switched on his torch.

The beds of heather and bracken were there as they had left them, and their macs and rugs and rucksacks. Nothing seemed to have been disturbed. Julian lit the candles on the mantelpiece and the dark little underground room came to life at once.

'What's the matter with Timmy?' asked George, coming down into the room. 'He's still growling. Timmy, what's up?'

'I expect he can smell that the others have been down here,' said Dick. 'Look at him sniffing all round. It's quite clear that *someone* has been here.'

'Anyone hungry?' asked Anne. 'I could do with some cake and biscuits.'

'Right,' said Julian, and opened the cupboard where they had put the food they had bought.

There was none there! Except for the crockery and one or two odds and ends that had been in the cupboard before, there was nothing. The bread had gone, the biscuits, the chocolate – everything!

'Blow!' said Julian, angrily. 'Look at that! The beasts! They've taken all our food – every bit. Not even a biscuit left. We were mad not to think they might do that!'

'Clever of them,' said Dick. 'They know we can't stay here long without food. It's a good way of chasing us out. It's too late to go and get any tonight, anyway – and if we go tomorrow for some, they'll do what they have come to do in their own good time . . . when we're not here.'

Everyone felt distinctly down in the dumps. They were hungry and tired, and a good meal would have made all the difference. Anne sank down on her bed of heather and sighed.

'I wish I'd left some chocolate in my rucksack,' she said. 'But I didn't leave any there at all. And poor Tim

– he's hungry too! Look at him sniffing in the cupboard and looking round at George. Tim, there's nothing for you. The cupboard is bare!'

'Where have those two wretches gone?' suddenly said Julian, fiercely. 'I'll tick them off! I'll tell them what I think of people who come and rifle cupboards and take away all the food.'

'Woof,' said Timmy, in full agreement.

Julian went angrily up the stairs. He wondered again where Maggie and Dirty Dick were. He went to the empty doorway and looked out. Then he saw where they were.

Two small tents had been put up under some thickly growing trees! So that's where the two were going to sleep. He debated whether or not to go and tell them what he thought of people who stole food. He decided that he would.

But when he got over to the tents with Timmy, there was no one there! Rugs were laid inside, and there was a primus stove and a kettle and other odds and ends. At the back of one tent was a pile of something, covered by a cloth.

Julian had a good look into each tent, and then went to see if he could find out where Maggie and Dirty Dick had gone. He saw them at last, walking through the trees. They must have gone for an evening stroll, he thought.

They didn't come back to the tents, but sat down by the lake. Julian gave up the thought of tackling them and went back to the others. Timmy was left behind, snuffling about happily.

'They've got tents,' Julian informed the others when he was back in the cellar room again. 'They're obviously staying put till they've got what they came for. They aren't in the tents – they're out by the lake.'

'Where's Timmy?' asked George. 'You shouldn't have left him behind, Ju. They might do something to him.'

'Here he is!' said Julian, as a familiar noise of claws clattering on the floor came to their ears. Timmy came down the stone steps and ran to George.

'He's got something in his mouth!' said George, in surprise. Timmy dropped it into her lap. She gave a yell.

'It's a tin of shortbread! Where did he get it from?'

Julian began to laugh. 'He must have taken it from one of the tents!' he said. 'I saw something covered up with a cloth in one tent – their food, I imagine! Well, well – tit for tat – they took our food and now Timmy is taking theirs!'

'Fair exchange is no robbery,' grinned Dick. 'Serves them right! I say – Tim's gone again!'

He was back in a minute with something large and paper-covered. It was a big cake! The four roared with laughter. 'Timmy! You're a wonder! You really are!'

Timmy was pleased at this praise. Off he went again and brought back a cardboard box in which was a fine pork-pie. The children could hardly believe their eyes.

'It's a miracle!' said Anne. 'Just as I had made up my mind to starve for hours! A pork-pie of all things! Let's have some.'

'Well, I have no second thoughts about it,' said Julian, firmly. 'They took our food and we deserve some of theirs. Good gracious – don't say Tim's gone again.'

He had! He was enjoying himself thoroughly. He arrived this time with a packet of ham, and the children couldn't *imagine* how he had stopped himself from eating some on the way.

'Fancy carrying it in his mouth and not even *tasting* a bit!' said Dick. 'Tim's a better person than I am. I'd just have to have had a lick.'

'I say – we ought to stop him now,' said Julian, as Timmy ran up the steps again, his tail wagging nineteen to the dozen. 'We're getting a bit too much in exchange!'

'Oh, do see what he brings back this time,' begged Anne. 'Then stop him.'

He came back carrying an old flour bag in which something had been packed. Timmy carried it cleverly by the neck so that nothing had fallen out. George undid the bag.

'Home-made scones – and buns,' she said. 'Timmy, you are very, very clever, and you shall have a wonderful supper. But you are not to go and take any more things, because we've got enough. See? No more. Lie down and be a good dog and eat your supper.'

Timmy was quite willing. He wolfed ham and scones and a slice of cake, and then he went up into the kitchen, jumped into the sink and lapped the water lying there. He then jumped down and went to the doorway to look out. He barked. Then he growled loudly.

The children rushed up the stone steps at once. Outside, at a safe distance, was Dirty Dick.

'Have you been taking anything of ours?' he shouted.

'No more than you have been taking of ours!' shouted back Julian. 'Fair exchange, you know, and all that.'

'How dare you go into our tents?' raged the man, his shock of hair making him look very peculiar in the twilight.

'We didn't. The dog fetched and carried for us,' said

Julian. 'And don't you come any nearer. He's just longing to fly at you! And I warn you, he'll be on guard tonight, so don't try any funny tricks. He's as strong and savage as a lion.'

'Grrrr,' said Timmy, so fiercely that the man started back in fright. He went off without another word, shaking with anger.

Julian and the others went back to finish a very delicious supper. Timmy went with them – but he planted himself at the top of the cellar steps.

'Not a bad place for him to be in tonight,' said Julian. 'I don't trust that couple an inch. We can give him one of our blazers to lie on. I say – this has boiled up into quite an adventure, hasn't it? It seems frightful to think we'll be back at school on Tuesday!'

'We *must* find the loot first!' said Anne. 'We really must. Let's get out that plan again, Ju. Let's make sure that Tall Stone is marked on it.'

They got it out and put it on the table. They bent over it once more.

'Yes – Tall Stone is marked at the end of one of the lines,' said Julian. 'Tock Hill is at the end of the opposite line. Let's get the map and see if there *is* a Tock Hill.'

They got the map, and studied it. Anne suddenly put her finger down on it. 'There it is. On the opposite side of the lake from where we saw the Tall Stone. Tock Hill on one side. Tall Stone on the other. Surely that *means* something.'

'It does, of course,' said Julian. 'It is bearings given to show the whereabouts of the hidden goods. There are four bearings given – Tall Stone. Tock Hill. Chimney. And Steeple.'

'Listen!' said Dick, suddenly. 'LISTEN! *I* know how to read that map. It's easy.'

The others looked at him in surprise and doubt.
'Read it, then,' said Julian. 'Tell us what it all means.
I don't believe you can!'

18 A very exciting time

'Let's take all the clues we know,' said Dick, looking excited. 'Two-Trees. That's here. Gloomy Water. That's where the hidden stuff must be. *Saucy Jane*. It's a boat that contains the stuff, hidden somewhere on Gloomy Water.'

'Go on,' said Julian, as Dick paused to think.

'Maggie is the next clue – well she's here, probably an old friend of Nailer's,' said Dick. 'She knows all the clues too.'

He jabbed his finger at the piece of paper. 'Now for *these* clues. Listen! We saw Tall Stone when we were out on the lake, didn't we? Very well. There must be SOME spot on the lake where we can see not only Tall Stone, but also Tock Hill, Chimney and Steeple, whatever they are! There must be only one spot from which we can see all those four things at the same time – and *that's* the spot to hunt in for the treasure!'

There was an astonished silence after this. Julian drew a long breath and clapped Dick on the back.

'Of course! What idiots we were not to see it before. The *Saucy Jane* must be somewhere on – or in – the lake at the spot where all four clues are seen at the same time. We've only got to explore and find out!'

'Yes – but don't forget that Maggie and Dirty Dick know what these clues mean too! They'll be there first if they possibly can!' said Dick. 'And what's more if they get the goods we can't do anything about it.

We're not the police! They'll be off and away with their find and disappear completely.'

Everyone began to feel intensely excited. 'I think we'd better set off early tomorrow morning,' said Julian. 'As soon as it's light. Otherwise Maggie and Dick will get in first. I wish to goodness we had an alarm clock.'

'We'll go on the raft, and we'll paddle about till we see Tall Stone again – then we'll keep that in sight till we see Tock Hill, whatever that is,' said Dick. 'And once we've spotted that we'll keep both Tall Stone *and* Tock Hill in sight and paddle round to find out where we can see a steeple – and then a chimney. I should think that would be the one chimney left on Two-Trees house! Did you notice there is just one left, sticking up high?'

'Yes, I noticed,' said Anne. 'What a clever way to hide anything, Dick. Nobody could possibly know what the clues meant unless they knew something of the secret. This is *awfully* exciting!'

They talked about it for some time and then Julian said they really must try and go to sleep or they would never wake up early enough in the morning.

They settled down in their beds of heather and bracken. Timmy lay on Julian's blazer on the top step of the stairs leading down to the cellar room. He seemed to think it was quite a good idea to sleep there that night.

They were all tired and they fell asleep very quickly. Nothing disturbed them in the night. The fox came again and looked into the old house, but Timmy didn't stir. He merely gave a small growl and the fox fled, his bushy tail spread behind him.

The morning came and daylight crept in at the burnt-out doorway and windows. Timmy stirred and went to the door. He looked towards the two tents. No one was about there. He went to the cellar steps and clattered down waking Dick and Julian at once.

'What's the time?' said Julian, remembering immediately that he was to wake early. 'Half past seven. Wake up, everyone! It's daylight. We've heaps to do!'

They washed hurriedly, combed out their hair, cleaned their teeth, and tried·to brush-down their clothes. Anne got ready some snacks for them – ham, scones and a piece of shortbread each. They all had a drink of water and then they were ready to go.

There was no sign of anyone near the two tents. 'Good,' said Julian. 'We'll be there first!'

They dragged the raft out and got on to it, taking up the paddles. Then off they went, Timmy too, all feeling tremendously excited.

'We'll paddle out to where we think we were last night when Anne caught sight of Tall Stone,' said Julian. So they paddled valiantly, though their arms were stiff with yesterday's paddling and it was really very painful to use the tired muscles all over again!

They paddled out to the middle of the lake and looked for Tall Stone. It didn't seem anywhere to be seen! They strained their eyes for it, but for a long time it was not to be spotted at all. Then Dick gave a cry. 'It's just come into sight. Look, when we passed those tall trees on the bank over there, Tall Stone came into view. It was behind them before that.'

'Good,' said Julian. 'Now I'm going to stop paddling and keep Tall Stone in sight. If it goes out of sight I'll tell you and you must back-paddle. Dick, can you possibly paddle and look out for something that could be Tock Hill on the opposite side? I daren't take my eyes off Tall Stone in case it disappears.'

'Right,' said Dick, and paddled while he looked earnestly for Tock Hill.

'Got it!' he said suddenly. 'It must be it! Look, over there – a funny little hill with a pointed top. Julian, can you still see Tall Stone?'

'Yes,' said Julian. 'Keep your eyes on Tock Hill. Now it's up to the girls. George, paddle away and see if you can spot Steeple.'

'I can see it now, already!' said George, and for one moment the boys took their eyes off Tall Stone and Tock Hill and looked where George pointed. They saw the steeple of a faraway church glinting in the morning sun.

'Good, good, good,' said Julian. 'Now Anne – look for Chimney – look down towards the end of the lake where the house is. Can you see its one chimney?'

'Not quite,' said Anne. 'Paddle just a bit to the left – the left, I said, George! Yes – yes, I can see the one chimney. Stop paddling everyone. We're here!'

They stopped paddling but the raft drifted on, and Anne lost the chimney again! They had to paddle back a bit until it came into sight. By that time George had lost her steeple!

At last all four things were in view at once, and the raft seemed to be still and unmoving on the quiet waters of the lake.

'I'm going to drop something to mark the place,' said Julian, still keeping his eyes desperately on Tall Stone. 'George, can you manage to watch Tall Stone and Steeple at the same time? I simply must look what I'm doing for the moment.'

'I'll try,' said George, and fixed her eyes first on Tall Stone, then on Steeple, then on Tall Stone again, hoping and praying that neither would slip out of sight if the raft moved on the water.

Julian was busy. He had taken his torch and his pocket-knife out of his pocket and had tied them together with string. 'I haven't enough string, Dick,' he said. 'You've got some, haven't you?'

Dick had, of course. He put his hand into his pocket, still keeping his eyes on Tock Hill and passed his string over to Julian.

Julian tied it to the end of the string that joined together the knife and torch. Then he dropped them into the water, letting out the string as they went down with their weight. The string slid through his hands. It stopped in a short while and Julian knew that the knife and torch had reached the bed of the lake.

He felt in his pockets again. He knew he had a cork somewhere that he had carved into a horse's head. He found it and tied the end of the string firmly round it. Then he dropped the cork thankfully into the water. It bobbed there, held by the string, which led right down to the knife and torch on the lake-bed below.

'It's done!' he said, with a sigh of relief. 'Take your eyes off everything! I've marked the place now, so we don't need to glue our eyes on the four bearings!'

He told them how he had tied together his knife and torch and dropped them on string to the bottom of the lake, and then had tied a cork to the other end, so that it would bob and show them the place.

They all looked at it. 'Jolly clever, Ju,' said Dick. 'But once we slide away from this spot, and it would be an easy thing to do, we'd find it jolly difficult to find that cork again! Hadn't we better tie something else to it?'

'I haven't got anything else that will float,' said Julian. 'Have you?'

'I have,' said George, and she handed him a little wooden box. 'I keep the five pence pieces I collect in that,' she said, putting the money into her pocket. 'You can have the box. It will be much easier to see than the cork.'

Julian tied the box to the cork. It was certainly a good deal easier to see! 'Fine!' he said. 'Now we're quite all right. We must be right over the loot!'

They all bent over the edge of the raft and looked down – and they saw a most surprising sight! Below them, resting on the bottom of the lake, was a boat! It lay there in the shadows of the water, its outline blurred by the ripples the raft made – but quite plainly it was a boat!

'The *Saucy Jane*!' said Julian, peering down, feeling amazed and awed to think that they had read the bearings so correctly that they were actually over the *Saucy Jane* herself! 'The Nailer must have come here with the stolen goods – got out the *Saucy Jane* and rowed her to this spot. He must have taken his bearings very carefully indeed, and then holed the boat so that she sank down with the loot in her. Then I suppose he swam back to shore.'

'Most ingenious,' said Dick. 'Really, he must be a jolly clever fellow. But I say, Julian – how on earth are we going to get the boat up?'

'I can't imagine,' said Julian. 'I simply – can't – imagine! I hadn't even thought of that.'

Timmy suddenly began to growl. The four looked up quickly to see why.

They saw a boat coming over the water towards them – the *Merry Meg*, with Maggie and Dirty Dick in it. And the children felt quite certain that both were reading the bearings on their piece of paper in exactly the same way as they themselves had!

They were so engrossed in watching for Tall Stone, Tock Hill, Chimney and Steeple that they took no notice of the children at all. 'I don't think they guess for one moment that we've read the bearings and marked the place,' said Julian. 'How wild they'll be when they find we are right over the place they're looking for! Watch out for trouble!'

19   Maggie and Dick are annoyed

The boat in which Maggie and Dirty Dick were rowing went this way and that as the two searched for the same objects that the children had already spotted. The four watched them, and George put her hand on Timmy to stop him barking.

The boat came nearer and nearer. Maggie was trying to keep in view two or three of the bearings at once and her head twisted from side to side continually. The children grinned at one another. It had been hard enough for the four of them to keep all the bearings in view – it must be very difficult for Maggie, especially as Dirty Dick didn't seem to be helping very much.

They heard Maggie give sharp orders as the boat swung this way and that. Then it headed for them. Dirty Dick growled something to Maggie, who had her back to them, and she turned round sharply, losing the view of the things she was looking for.

Her face was full of anger when she saw the raft so near – and in the place where she wanted *her* boat to go! Afraid of completely losing the view of the things she was keeping her eyes on, she turned back again and hastily looked to see if Tock Hill, Tall Stone and Steeple were still all to be seen together. She said something in a furious voice to Dirty Dick, and he nodded with a sour face.

The boat came nearer and they heard Maggie say 'I

think I can see it now – yes – a bit farther to the right, please.'

'She's spotted one Chimney now,' whispered Anne. 'I expect they've got all the bearings. Oh dear – the boat will bump right into us!'

It did! Dirty Dick rowed viciously at them and the bows of the boat gave them a terrific jolt. Anne would have fallen into the water if Julian hadn't grabbed at her.

He yelled at Dirty Dick. 'Look out, you ass! You nearly had us over! What on earth do you think you're doing?'

'Get out of the way then,' growled Dirty Dick. Timmy began to bark savagely, and the boat at once drew away from the raft.

'There's plenty of room on this lake,' shouted Julian. 'What do you want to come and disturb us for? We aren't doing any harm.'

'We're going to report you to the police,' called the woman, her face red with anger. 'Taking a raft that doesn't belong to you, sleeping in a house where you've no right to be – and stealing our food.'

'Don't talk nonsense,' cried Julian. 'And don't you dare to ram us again. If you do I'll send our dog after you. He's longing to come.'

'Grrrr!' said Timmy, and showed his magnificent set of gleaming white teeth. Dirty Dick muttered something quickly to Maggie. She turned round again and called to them.

'Now look here, you kids – be sensible. My friend and I have come down here for a quiet weekend, and it isn't nice to find you four everywhere we go. Go back and keep out of our way and we won't report you at all. That's a fair bargain – we won't even say anything about your stealing our food.'

'We're going back when we think we will,' answered Julian. 'And no threats or bargains will make any difference to us.'

There was a silence. Then Maggie spoke hurriedly to Dirty Dick again. He nodded.

'Is this your half-term?' she called. 'When do you have to go back?'

'Tomorrow,' said Julian. 'You'll be rid of us then. But we're going to enjoy ourselves on this raft while we can.'

There was another hurried conference between the two. Then Dirty Dick rowed round a little, and Maggie began to peer down into the water. She suddenly looked up, nodded at Dirty Dick, and he rowed away again towards the end of the lake! Not another word did the couple say.

'I can see what they've decided to do,' said Julian, in a pleased voice. 'They think we'll be gone by tomorrow, so they'll wait till the coast is clear and then they'll come and collect the loot in peace. Did you see Maggie looking down into the water to spot the boat? I was afraid she would also spot our mark – the cork and the box! But she didn't.'

'I don't know why you sound so pleased,' said George. 'We can't get the boat up, you know that – and *I* don't feel pleased that we'll have to leave tomorrow and let that horrid pair collect the loot. I imagine they'll have some clever grown-up way of pulling up the boat from the bed of the lake – which they will do when we've gone tomorrow.'

'You're not very bright today, George,' said Julian, watching the boat being rowed farther and farther away. 'I told them we'd be gone tomorrow, hoping they would clear off and wait – and leave us time to get the loot ourselves. I think we can!'

'How?' said three voices at once, and Timmy looked inquiringly at Julian too.

'Well, we don't need to pull up the *boat*,' said Julian. 'We only want the loot. What's to prevent us from going down and getting it? I'm quite prepared to strip and dive down to the bottom there and feel about for any sack or bag or box. If I find one I'll come up for air, borrow a bit of rope from the raft and go down again – tie the rope to the sack and you can haul it up to the surface!'

'Oh Julian – it sounds so easy – but is it really?' said Anne. George and Dick considered the proposal carefully. They were most impressed by Julian's idea.

'Well, it may turn out to be much more difficult than it sounds, but I'm jolly well going to try it,' said Julian, and began to strip off his jersey.

Anne felt the water. It was very cold to her warm hand. 'Ugh! I'd hate to dive down to the bottom of this horrid cold dark lake,' she said. 'I think you're brave, Ju.'

'Don't talk rubbish!' said Julian.

He was ready to go in now. He dived neatly into the water with hardly a splash. The other three craned over the edge of the raft to watch. They could see him down, deep down in the water, a ghostly figure. He stayed down such a long time that Anne got worried.

'He can't hold his breath all that time!' she said. 'He can't!'

But Julian could. He was one of the star swimmers and divers at his school, and this was easy to him. He came up again at last, and panted hard, trying to make up for holding his breath so long. The others waited patiently. At last his breathing grew more even and he grinned at them.

'Ah – that's better! Well – it's there!' he said, triumphantly.

'*Is* it!' said everyone, thrilled. 'Oh Julian!'

'Yes. I dived right down to the boat – almost got there with the force of my dive – had to swim just a couple of strokes perhaps. And there was the poor old boat, rotting to bits. And in one end is a waterproof bag – almost a sack, it's so big. I ran my hands over it, and it's waterproof all right – so the loot must be packed in there.'

'Did it feel heavy?' asked Dick.

'I gave it a tug and couldn't move it,' said Julian. 'Either it's wedged in somehow or is really heavy. Anyway we can't fetch it out by diving down for it. I'll have to dive down again, fix a rope to it, then come up – and we'll give a heave-ho and up she'll come!'

Julian was shivering. Anne picked up the blazer she had brought and gave it to him to dry himself with. Dick looked hurriedly over the raft. There were certainly bits and pieces of rope sticking out here and there, some of it half-rotten; and a short length was tucked into a space between two planks of the raft.

It was much too short though – and surely the other bits and pieces would never join to make a long enough rope?

'The bits of rope we've got won't do, Julian,' said Dick. Julian was drying himself and looking towards the end of the lake, where Two-Trees stood. He was frowning. The others looked too.

The boat had reached the bank there, and had been pulled up. One of the couple, the children couldn't see which, was standing up on the bank – and something was glinting in the sun, something he or she was holding!

'See that glint?' said Julian. 'Well, that's either

Maggie or Dirty Dick using field-glasses. They're going to keep an eye on us while we're here – just to make
sure we don't suddenly spot the boat, I suppose! They
don't guess we've already found it. I bet they were
worried when they saw I'd taken a header into the
water just over the sunken boat!'

'Oh – so that's what the flash is,' said George. 'The
glint of field-glasses! Yes – they're watching us. Blow!
That will put an end to us trying to haul up the loot, Ju.
They'd see it and wait for us!'

'Yes. No good trying for that now,' said Julian.
'Anyway, as Dick says, we've not got enough rope.
We'll have to get some from the boat-house.'

'But when do you propose to get the bag out of the
sunken boat?' asked Dick. 'They'll keep those field-
glasses on us even if we go out again this afternoon.'

'There's only one time to go when they *won't* have
their glasses watching us,' said Julian, beginning to
dress himself very rapidly, 'and that's tonight. We'll
go tonight! My word – what an adventure!'

'Don't let's,' said Anne, in a small voice.

'There'll be a moon,' said George, excited.

'Smashing idea!' said Dick, thumping Julian on the
back. 'Let's go back now so that they won't have any
suspicions of us, and make our plans for tonight. And
we'd better keep an eye on them too in case they row
out to this spot themselves this afternoon.'

'They won't,' said Julian. 'They daren't run any risk
of us spotting what they're doing. They will be sure to
wait till we've gone.'

'And till the loot is gone!' said George with a laugh.
'I say – I do hope those two wretches haven't gone and
taken our food again!'

'I hid it down in the cellars beyond our room – and
locked the door leading there – and here's the key,'

grinned Julian, holding up a large key.

'You never told us!' said George. 'Julian, you're a genius! How do you manage to think of things like that?'

'Oh – just brains!' said Julian, pretending to look modest, and then laughing. 'Come on – if I don't get warm quickly I'll have a most almighty chill!'

20   In the moonlight

They paddled rapidly away. Dick took a last glance back to make sure that the cork and the box were still bobbing on the water to mark the place where the sunken boat lay. Yes – they were still there.

'It'll be maddening if it's cloudy tonight and the moon doesn't come out,' said George, as they paddled. 'We shouldn't be able to see Tock Hill, Tall Stone and the rest – and we might paddle for ages in the dark without spotting our cork-and-box mark.'

'Don't cross your bridges before you come to them,' said Dick.

'I'm not,' said George. 'I was only just *hoping* that wouldn't happen.'

'It won't,' said Julian, looking at the sky. 'The weather's set fine again.'

As soon as Maggie saw the children coming back again, she and Dirty Dick disappeared into their tents. Julian grinned. 'They've heaved a sigh of relief and gone to have a snack,' he said. 'I could do with one myself.'

Everyone felt the same. Paddling was hard work, and the air on the lake was chilly – quite enough to give anyone a large appetite!

They pushed the raft into its hiding-place again. Then they made their way to the old house. They went down into the cellar room. Timmy growled and sniffed about again.

'I bet Maggie and Dirty Dick have been here, snooping round again,' said George. 'Looking for their pork-pie and ham! Good thing you locked it up, Ju!'

Julian unlocked the door into the cellars beyond, and brought out the food. 'A large toad was looking at it with great interest,' he said, as he brought it back. 'Timmy also looked at the toad with interest – but he's wary of toads by now. They taste much too nasty when pounced on!'

They took the meal up into the sunshine and enjoyed it. The orangeade was finished so they drank the cold clear water, pumping some vigorously.

'Do you know it's a quarter to three?' said Julian amazed. 'Where has the time gone? In a couple of hours or so it will be dark. Let me see – the moon will be well up about eleven o'clock. That's the time to go, I think.'

'Please don't let's,' said Anne. Julian put his arm round her.

'Now you know you don't mean that, Anne,' he said. 'You know you'll enjoy it all when the time comes. You couldn't bear to be left out of it! Could you?'

'No. I suppose I couldn't,' said Anne. 'But I *don't* like Maggie and Dirty Dick!'

'Nor do we,' said Julian, cheerfully. 'That's why we're going to beat them at their own game. We're on the side of the right, and it's worthwhile running into a bit of danger for that. Now let's see – perhaps we'd better just keep an eye on that couple till it's dark – just in *case* they try any funny tricks – and then we'll have a snooze, if we can, so as to be sure to be lively tonight.'

'There they are!' said Anne. As she spoke Maggie and her companion came out of their tents. They had a few words together and then walked off to the moorland.

'Taking their usual stroll, I suppose,' said Dick. 'Let's have a game of cricket. There's a bit of wood over there for a bat, and I've got a ball in my rucksack.'

'Good idea,' said Julian. 'I still feel a bit chilled from my bathe. Brrrrrr! That water was cold. I don't feel very thrilled at the thought of diving in tonight!'

'I'll do that,' said Dick, at once. 'My turn this time!'

'No. I know exactly where to spot the loot,' said Julian. 'I'll have to go down. But you can come down too, if you like, and help to tie the rope on to it.'

'Right,' said Dick. 'Now look out – I'm going to bowl!'

They enjoyed their game. The sun sank lower and lower, then it disappeared. A cloud came over the sky and darkness came quickly. George looked up at the sky anxiously.

'It's all right,' said Julian. 'It'll clear. Don't you worry!'

Before they went back into the house Julian and Dick slipped down to the boat-house for the coil of rope they would want that night. They found it quite easily enough and came back, pleased. It was quite a good strong rope, frayed only in one place.

Julian was right about the weather. The sky cleared again in about an hour, and the stars shone crisply. Good! Julian put Timmy on guard at the doorway. Then he and the others went into the dark cellar room and lit a couple of candles. They all snuggled down into their beds of heather.

'I shan't be able to snooze,' complained Anne. 'I feel much too excited.'

'Don't snooze then,' said Dick. 'Just have a rest and wake us up at the right time!'

Anne was the only one who didn't fall into a comfortable doze. She lay awake, thinking of this new adventure of theirs. Some children always had adventures and some didn't. Anne thought it would be much nicer to *read* about adventures than to have them. But then probably the ones who only read about them simply longed to have the adventures themselves! It was all very difficult.

Anne woke the others at ten to eleven. She shook George first, and then the boys. They were all in such a comfortable sleep that it was hard to wake them.

But soon they were up and about, whispering. 'Where's the rope? Good, here it is. Better put on blazers *and* macs. It'll be freezing on the lake. Everyone ready? Now – not a sound!'

Timmy had come to the cellar room as soon as he had heard them stirring. He knew he had to be quiet so he didn't give even one small bark. He was thrilled to find they were going out into the night.

The moon was well up now, and although it was not full, it was very bright. Small clouds swam across the sky, and every now and again the moon went behind one of them and the world became dark. But that was only for a minute or two, then out it came again, as brilliant as ever.

'Any sign of the others?' whispered Dick. Julian stood at the doorway and looked towards the tents. No – all was quiet there. Still, it would be better if he and the others crept round the side of the house and kept in the shadows.

'We don't want to run any risk of them spotting us now,' whispered Julian, giving his orders. 'Keep out of the moonlight, whatever you do. And see that Tim walks to heel, George.'

Keeping well in the shadows the five crept down to

the lake-side. The water gleamed in the moonlight, and a bright moon-path ran all down it, lovely to see. The lake looked very dark and brooding. Anne wished it had a voice of some kind – even the little lap-lap-lap of waves at the edge. But there was none.

They pulled out the raft and threw the coil of rope on to it. Then they clambered on, enjoying its smooth bob-bob-bobbing as they paddled out on the water. They were off!

Timmy was thrilled. He kept licking first one of the four, then another. He loved going out in the night. The moon shone down on the little company and turned every little ripple to silver as the raft bobbed over the water.

'It's a heavenly night,' said Anne, looking round at the silent trees that lined the banks. 'The whole place is so quiet and peaceful.'

An owl immediately hooted very loudly indeed from the trees and Anne jumped violently.

'Now don't start all the owls hooting by talking about how quiet everything is,' teased Julian. 'I agree though that it really is a heavenly evening. How calm and mirror-like this lake is. I wonder if it ever produces a wave of any sort! Do you suppose it stays like this even in a storm?'

'It's a weird sort of lake,' said Dick. 'Look out, Timmy – that's my ear. Don't lick it all away. I say – anyone looking out for our four bearings?'

'Well, we know more or less where we've got to paddle the raft to,' said Julian. 'We'll go in that direction and then see if we're spotting the bearings. I'm sure we're going right at the moment.'

They were. George soon saw Tall Stone, and then Tock Hill came into sight. It wasn't long before Steeple was seen too, shining in the moonlight.

'I bet the Nailer came and hid his loot out here on a moonlit night,' said Julian. 'All the bearings can be seen so very clearly – even Tall Stone. We really must find out sometime what it is. It looks like a great stone pointer of some sort, put up in memory of something or somebody.'

'There's the Chimney now,' said Anne. 'We have got them all in view – we should be near our mark.'

'We are!' said Dick, pointing to a little dark bobbing thing nearby. 'The cork and the box. How extremely clever we are! I really have a great admiration for the Five!'

'Idiot!' said Julian. 'Go on, strip now, Dick – we'll do our job straight away. Brrrrrrr! It's cold!'

Both boys stripped quickly, putting their clothes into a neat pile in the middle of the raft. 'Look after them, Anne,' said Julian. 'Got the rope, Dick? Come on, then, in we go. We can't see the boat now, the waters are so dark – but we know it's just below the cork and the box!'

The boys dived in one after the other. Splash! Splash! They were both beautiful divers. The raft rocked as they plunged in and Timmy nearly went in too.

Julian had dived in first. He opened his eyes under the water and found that he could see the sunken boat just below him. With two strong strokes he reached it, and tugged at the waterproof bag there. Dick was beside him almost at once, the rope in his hands. The boys twisted it tightly round the top part of the bag.

Before they could finish the job they had to rise up to the surface to breathe. Dick couldn't hold his breath under water as long as Julian and he was up first, gasping painfully. Then Julian shot up and the night was full of great, painful breaths, as the boys gasped in the air they longed for.

The girls knew better than to ask anything just then. They waited anxiously till the boys' breathing grew easier. Julian turned and grinned at them.

'Everything's all right!' he said. 'Now – down we go again!'

21 The sack at last!

Down went the boys again and once more the raft jerked violently. The girls peered anxiously over the edge, waiting for them to return.

Julian and Dick were down at the sunken boat in a matter of a second or two. They finished the task of tying the rope to the waterproof bag. Julian gave it a hard jerk, hoping to free it if it were wedged tightly into the boat. He took the rest of the rope length in his hands in order to take it up to the surface.

Then, bursting for breath again, the two boys shot up to the raft, popping out of the water with loud gasps. They climbed on board.

They took a minute to get their breath and then Dick and Julian took the rope together. The girls watched, their hearts beating fast. Now was the test! Would that waterproof sack come up – or not?

The boys pulled strongly but without jerking. The raft slanted and Anne made a grab at the pile of clothes in the middle. Dick fell off into the water again.

He climbed back, spluttering. 'Have to pull more smoothly,' he said. 'I felt the sack give a bit, didn't you?'

Julian nodded. He was shivering with cold, but his eyes were shining with excitement. Anne put a macintosh round his shoulders and one round Dick's too. They never even noticed!

'Now – pull again,' said Julian. 'Steady does it –

steady – steady! It's coming! Gosh, it's really coming. Pull, Dick, pull!'

As the heavy bag came up on the end of the rope, the raft slanted again, and the boys pushed themselves back to the other side of the raft, afraid of upsetting everyone into the water. Timmy began to bark excitedly.

'Be quiet, Timmy,' said George at once. She knew how easily sound travels over water, and she was afraid the couple in the tents might hear him.

'It's coming – it's there, look – just below the surface!' said Anne. 'One more pull, boys!'

But it was impossible to pull the heavy bag on board without upsetting the raft. As it was, the girls got very wet when the water splashed over the raft as it jerked and slanted.

'Look – let's paddle back to the shore and let the sack drag behind us,' said Julian, at last. 'We shall only upset the raft. Dress again, Dick, and we'll get back to the old house and open the sack in comfort. I'm so cold now that I can harldy feel my fingers.'

The boys dressed as quickly as they could. They were shivering, and were very glad to take up their paddles and work hard to get the raft back to shore. They soon felt a welcome warmth stealing through their bodies, and in ten minutes had stopped shivering. They felt very pleased with themselves indeed.

They looked back at the bulky object following them, dragging along just under the surface. What was in that bag? Excitement crept over all of them again, and the paddles struck through the water at top speed as all the four strained to get back as quickly as possible. Timmy felt the excitement too, and wagged his long tail without ceasing as he stood in the middle

of the raft, watching the thing that bobbed along
behind them.

They came at last to the end of the lake. Making as
little noise as possible they dragged the raft under its
usual bush. They did not want to leave it out on the
bank in case Maggie and Dirty Dick saw that it had
been used again, and started wondering.

Dick and Julian dragged the waterproof sack out of
the water. They carried it between them as they went
cautiously back to the house. It looked a most miserable, grotesque place with its burnt-out roof, door-
ways and windows – but the children didn't notice its
forlorn appearance in the moonlight – they were far
too excited!

They walked slowly up the overgrown path between the two broken-down walls, their feet making no sound on the soft mossy ground. They came
to the doorway and dragged the bundle into the
kitchen.

'Go and light the candles in the cellar room,' said
Julian to George. 'I just want to make sure that that
couple are not snooping anywhere about.'

George and Anne went to light the candles, flashing
their torches before them down the stone steps. Julian
and Dick stood at the open doorway, facing the moonlight, listening intently. Not a sound was to be heard,
not a shadow moved!

They set Timmy on guard and left him there,
dragging the dripping, heavy bundle across the stone
floor of the kitchen. They bumped it down the cellar
steps – and at last had it before them, ready to be
opened!

Julian's fingers fumbled at the knots of the rope.
George couldn't bear waiting. She took a pocket-knife
and handed it to Julian.

'For goodness' sake, cut the rope!' she said. 'I simply can't wait another moment.'

Julian grinned. He cut the rope – and then he looked to see how to undo the waterproof wrapping.

'I see,' he said. 'It's been folded over and over the goods, and then sewn up to make a kind of bag. It must have kept the loot absolutely waterproof.'

'Buck *up!*' said George. 'I shall tear it open myself in a minute!'

Julian cut the strong stitches that closed the covering. They began to unwrap the bundle. There seemed to be yards and yards of waterproof covering! But at last it was off – and there, in the middle of the mass of waterproof, were scores of little boxes – leather-covered boxes that everyone knew at once were jewel-boxes!

'It *is* jewellery then!' said Anne, and she opened a box. They all exclaimed in wonder.

A magnificent necklace glittered on black velvet. It shone and glinted and sparkled in the candlelight as if it were on fire. Even the two boys gazed without a word. Why – it was fit for a queen!

'It must be that wonderful necklace stolen from the Queen of Fallonia,' said George at last. 'I saw a picture of it in the papers. What diamonds!'

'Oooh – are they *diamonds!*' said Anne, in awe. 'Oh Julian – what a lot of money they must be worth! A hundred pounds, do you think?'

'A hundred thousand pounds more likely, Anne,' said Julian, soberly. 'My word – no wonder the Nailer hid these stolen goods carefully, in such an ingenious place. No wonder Maggie and Dirty Dick were longing to find them. Let's see what else there is.'

Every box contained precious stones of some kind – sapphire bracelets, ruby and diamond rings, a strange and wonderful opal necklace, earrings of such enormous diamonds that Anne was quite sure no one would be able to bear the weight of them!

'I would never, never dare to own jewellery like this,' said Anne. 'I should always be afraid of its being stolen. Did it all belong to the Queen of Fallonia?'

'No. Some to a princess who was visiting her,' said Julian. 'These jewels are worth a king's ransom. I just hate the thought of being in charge of them, even for a little while.'

'Well, it's better that we should have them, rather than Maggie or Dirty Dick,' said George. She held a string of diamonds in her hands and let them run through her fingers. How they sparkled! No one could have imagined that they had been at the bottom of a lake for a year or two!

'Now let's see,' said Julian, sitting down on the edge of the table. 'We're due back at school tomorrow afternoon, Tuesday – or is it Tuesday already? It must be past midnight – gosh, yes, it's almost half past two! Would you believe it?'

'I feel as if I'd believe anything,' said Anne, blinking at the glittering treasure on the table.

'We'd better start off fairly early tomorrow,' went on Julian. 'We've got to get these things to the police . . .'

'*Not* to that awful policeman we saw the other day!' said George, in horror.

'Of course not. I think our best course would be to ring up that nice Mr Gaston and tell him that we've got important news for the police and see which police station he recommends us to go to,' said Julian. 'He might even arrange a car for us, so that we don't need to take this stuff about in buses. I'm not particularly keen on carrying it about with me!'

'Have we got to carry all these boxes?' said George, in dismay.

'No. That would be asking for trouble if anyone spotted them,' said Julian. 'I fear we'll just have to wrap up the jewels in our hankies and stuff them down into the bottom of our rucksacks. We'll leave the boxes here. The police can collect them afterwards if they want to.'

It was all decided. The four divided up the glittering jewellery and wrapped it carefully into four handkerchiefs, one for each of them. They stuffed the hankies into their rucksacks.

'We'd better use them for pillows,' said Dick. 'Then they'll be quite safe.'

'What! These horrid rough bags!' said Anne. 'Why? Timmy's on guard, isn't he? I'll put mine beside me under the rug but I just won't put my head on it.'

Dick laughed. 'All right, Anne. Timmy won't let any robber through, I'm quite sure. Now – we start off first thing in the morning, do we, Julian?'

'Yes. As soon as we wake,' said Julian. 'We can't have much to eat. There're only a few biscuits and a bit of chocolate left.'

'*I* shan't mind,' said Anne. 'I'm so excited that at the moment I don't feel I'll ever eat anything again!'

'You'll change your mind tomorrow,' said Julian with a laugh. 'Now – to bed, everyone.'

They lay down on their heather and bracken, excited and pleased. What a weekend! And all because Dick and Anne had lost their way and Dick slept in the wrong barn!

'Good-night,' said Julian, yawning. 'I feel very very rich – richer than I'll ever be in my life again. Well – I'll enjoy the feeling while I can!'

22 An exciting finish

They awoke to hear Timmy barking. It was daylight already. Julian leapt up the steps to see what was the matter. He saw Maggie not very far away.

'Why do you keep such a fierce dog?' she called. 'I just came to see if you wanted to take any food with you. We'll give you some if you like.'

'It's *too* kind of you, all of a sudden!' said Julian. How anxious Maggie was to get rid of them! She would even give them food to get rid of them quickly. But Julian didn't want any food from Maggie or Dirty Dick!

'Do you want some, then?' asked the woman. She couldn't make Julian out. He looked a youngster, and yet his manner was anything but childish. She was rather afraid of him.

'No thanks,' said Julian. 'We're just about to go. Got to get back to school today, you know.'

'Well, you'd better hurry then,' said the woman. 'It's going to rain.'

Julian turned on his heel, grinning. It wasn't going to rain. Maggie would say anything to hurry them away! Still, that was just what Julian wanted – to get away as quickly as possible!

In ten minutes' time the four children were ready to go. Each had rucksack and mac on their backs – and each had jewels worth thousands of pounds in their charge! What a very extraordinary thing.

'It will be a lovely walk across the moors,' said Anne, as they went along. 'I feel like singing now everything's turned out all right. The only thing is – nobody at school will believe George or me when we tell them what's happened.'

'We shall probably be set a composition to do – "What did you do on your half-term?"' said George. 'And Miss Peters will read ours and say "Quite well-written, but *rather* far-fetched, don't you think?"'

Everyone laughed. Timmy looked round with his tongue out and what George called 'his *smiling* face'. Then his 'smile' vanished, and he began to bark, facing to the rear of the children.

They looked round, startled. 'Gosh – it's Maggie and Dirty Dick – rushing along like fury!' said Dick. 'What's up? Are they sorry we've gone and want us back again?'

'They're trying to cut us off,' said Julian. 'Look – they've left the path and they're going to take a short cut to come across us. There is marshland all round, so we can't leave our own path. What idiots they are! Unless they know this bit of marsh-moor country they'll get bogged.'

Maggie and Dirty Dick were yelling and shouting in a fury. Dirty Dick shook his fists, and leapt from tuft to tuft like a goat.

'They look as if they have gone quite mad,' said Anne, suddenly afraid. 'What's the matter with them?'

'I know!' said George. 'They've been into our cellar room – and they've found that waterproof covering and all those empty boxes. They've found out that we've got the goods!'

'Of course!' said Julian. 'We should have thrown all the boxes into the cellars beyond. No wonder they're in a fury. They've lost a fortune to us four!'

'What do they think they can do now, though?' said Dick. 'We've got Timmy. He'll certainly fly at them if they come too near. But Dirty Dick looks mad enough to fight even Timmy. Honestly, I think he's gone off his head.'

'I think he has,' said Julian, startled by the man's mad shouts and behaviour.

He looked at Anne, who had gone white. Julian felt sure that Timmy would go for Dirty Dick and bring him to the ground, and he didn't want Anne to see dog and man fighting savagely. There was no doubt that Dirty Dick was quite out of his mind with rage and disappointment.

Timmy began to bark fiercely. He snarled, and looked very savage. He could see that the man was spoiling for a fight with someone. All right – Timmy didn't mind!

'Let's hurry on,' said Julian. 'But no short cuts for us, mind – we'll keep strictly to the path. Maggie is in difficulties already.'

So she was. She was floundering ankle deep in marshy ground, yelling to Dirty Dick to help her. But he was too intent on cutting right across the children's path.

And then *he* got into difficulties too! He suddenly sank up to his knees! He tried to clamber out and reach a tuft of some sort. He missed his footing and went down again. He gave an anguished yell. 'My ankle! I've broken it! Maggie, come over here!'

But Maggie was having her own difficulties and paid no attention. The children stopped and looked at Dirty Dick. He was sitting on a tuft, nursing his foot, and even from where the children stood they could see that his face was deathly white. He certainly had done something to his ankle.

'Ought we to help him?' said Anne, trembling.

'Good gracious no!' said Julian. 'He may be pretend-ing for all we know – though I don't think so. The chase is over, anyway. And if, as I think, Dirty Dick really has injured his ankle, he won't be able to get far out of that marsh – and nor will Maggie by the look of her – down she goes again, look! It may be that the police will find it very easy to pick up that unpleasant couple when they come along to look for them.'

'Nicely embedded in the marsh,' said Dick. 'Well, personally, I don't feel sorry for either of them. They're bad lots.'

They went on their way again, Timmy gloomy because he hadn't had a fight with Dirty Dick after all. They walked all the way to Reebles. It took them two hours.

'We'll go to the post-office, and telephone from there,' said Julian.

The old man was pleased to see them again. 'Had a nice time?' he said. 'Did you find Two-Trees?'

Julian left him talking to the others while he went to look up Mr Gaston's telephone number. He found it – and hoping devoutly that Mr Gaston wouldn't mind giving his help, he rang him up.

Mr Gaston answered the telephone himself. 'Hallo? Who? Oh, yes, of course I remember you. You want a bit of help? Well, what can I do for you?'

Julian told him. Mr Gaston listened in amazement. 'WHAT? You've found the Fallonia jewels! I can't believe it! In your rucksacks now, you say! Bless us all! You're not spoofing me, are you?'

Julian assured him that he wasn't. Mr Gaston could hardly believe his ears. 'Right. Right – of course I'll put you in touch with the police. We'd better go to Gathercombe – I know the inspector there, a fine fellow. Where are you? Oh yes, I know it. Wait there and I'll fetch you in my car – in about half an hour, say.'

He rang off and Julian went to find the others, delighted that he had thought of getting in touch with Mr Gaston. Some grown-ups were so jolly decent – and they knew exactly what to do. The other three were delighted too, when he told them.

'Well, I must say that although it's nice to have things happening to us, it's a sort of safe, comfortable feeling when we hand over to the grown-ups,' said George. 'Now I only want one thing – breakfast!'

'We'd better have a mixture of breakfast and lunch,' said Julian. 'It's so late.'

'Oh yes – let's have brunch!' said Anne, delighted. 'I love brunch.'

So they had some 'brunch' – sandwiches, buns, biscuits and ginger-beer, which they bought at a little shop down the road. And just as they were finishing, up swept Mr Gaston in an enormous car!

The four children grinned at him with pleasure. Julian introduced Anne and Dick. Timmy was thrilled to see him again and offered him a polite paw, which Mr Gaston shook heartily.

'Nice manners your dog's got,' he said, and pressed down the accelerator. Whooooosh! Away they went at top speed, with Timmy sticking his head out of the window as he always did in a car.

They told their extraordinary story as they went. Mr Gaston was full of admiration for all they had done. 'You're a bunch of plucky kids!' he kept saying. 'My word, I wish you were mine!'

They came to the police station. Mr Gaston had already warned the inspector they were coming, and he was waiting for them.

'Come along into my private room,' he said. 'Now first of all – where are these jewels? have you really got them with you? Let's have a look at them before you tell your story.'

The children undid their rucksacks – and out of the hankies inside they poured the shining, glittering jewellery on to the oak table.

The inspector whistled and exchanged a look with Mr Gaston. He picked up the diamond necklace.

'You've got them!' he said. 'The very jewels! And to think the police everywhere have been hunting for them for months and months and months. Where did you find them, youngsters?'

'It's rather a long story,' said Julian. He began to tell it, and he told it well, prompted by the others, when he forgot anything. Mr Gaston and the inspector listened with amazement on their faces. When Julian came to the bit where Dirty Dick and Maggie had been left floundering in the marshes, the inspector interrupted him.

'Wait! Would they still be there? They would? Right. Half a minute!'

He pressed a bell and a policeman appeared. 'Tell Johns to take his three men and the car, and go to the Green Marshes, near Gloomy Water,' ordered the inspector. 'He's to pick up two people floundering there – man and woman. Our old friends Dirty Dick and Maggie Martin! Look sharp!'

The policeman disappeared. Anne hugged herself. Now that awful couple would be put into safe custody for some time, thank goodness – till she had forgotten about them! Anne hadn't liked them a bit.

Julian's tale came to an end. The inspector looked across at the tousle-headed, dirty, untidy group and smiled. He held out his hand. 'Shake!' he said. 'All of

you!' You're the kind of kids we want in this country –
plucky, sensible, responsible youngsters who use your
brains and never give up! I'm proud to meet you!'

They all shook hands with him solemnly. Timmy
held up his paw too, and the inspector grinned and
shook that too.

'And now – what's your programme?' asked Mr
Gaston, getting up.

'Well – we're supposed to be back at school by three
o'clock,' said Julian. 'But I don't think we can arrive
looking like this. We'd get into awful rows! Is there a
hotel where we can have a bath and clean ourselves up
a bit?'

'You can do that here,' said the inspector. 'And if
you like I'll run you back to your schools in the police
car. We can't do too much for people who produce the
Fallonia jewels out of rucksacks, you know. Bless us
all – I can't believe it!'

Mr Gaston said good-bye and went, saying that he
was very proud to have made friends with them. 'And
don't you get stuck down any more rabbit-holes!' he
said to Timmy, who woofed happily at him.

They bathed and washed every inch of themselves.
They found their clothes neatly folded and brushed,
and felt grateful. They brushed their hair and arrived
looking very clean and tidy in the inspector's private
room. He had a man there, inspecting the jewels and
labelling them before he put them away into boxes.

'You'll be interested to know that we have picked
up your couple,' he told them. 'The man had a broken
ankle and couldn't stir a step. The woman was thigh
deep in the marsh when we found her. They quite
welcomed the police, they were so fed up with everything!'

'Oh *good*!' said the four, and Anne beamed with

relief. That settled Maggie and Dirty Dick then!

'And these *are* the Fallonia jewels,' said the inspector. 'Not that I had any doubt of it. They are now
being checked and labelled. I've no doubt the Queen of
Fallonia and her titled friend will be extremely pleased
to hear of your little exploit.'

A clock struck half past two. Julian looked at it. Half
an hour only to get back in time. Would they do it?

'It's all right,' said the inspector, with his wide grin.
'Car's at the door. I'll come and see you off. You'll all
be back at your schools in good time – and if anyone
believes your tale I'll be surprised. Come along!'

He saw them into the car, Timmy too. 'Good-bye,'
he said, and saluted them all smartly. 'I'm proud to
have met you – good luck to you, Famous Five!'

Yes, good luck to you, Famous Five – and may you
have many more adventures!

The Enid Blyton Newsletter

Would you like to receive The Enid Blyton Newsletter? It has lots of news about Enid Blyton books, videos, plays, etc. There are also puzzles and a page for your letters. It is published three times a year and is free for children who live in the United Kingdom and Ireland.

If you would like to receive it for a year, please write to: The Enid Blyton Newsletter, PO Box 357, London, WC2N 6QB, sending your name and address. (UK and Ireland only)

A complete list of the FAMOUS FIVE ADVENTURES by Enid Blyton

A complete list of the SECRET SEVEN ADVENTURES by Enid Blyton